The Great American Novel

Selected Visual Poetry (2001-2019)

Eileen R. Tabios

Paloma Press, 2019

Copyright © 2019 Eileen R. Tabios

Cover Image of "The Great American Novel" by Eileen R. Tabios

Cover & Book Design by C. Sophia Ibardaloza

ISBN 978-1-7323025-7-0

Library of Congress Control Number: 2018955873

No part of this book may be reproduced or transmitted in any form or by any means, electronic or mechanical, including photocopying, recording, or by any information storage and retrieval system, without permission in writing from the author or publisher.

ALSO FROM PALOMA PRESS:

Blue (poetry) by Wesley St. Jo & Remé Grefalda
Manhattan: An Archaeology (poetry) by Eileen R. Tabios
Marawi (chapbook) by Albert E. Alejo & Eileen R. Tabios, trans. by Aileen Cassinetto
After Irma After Harvey (chapbook) by Ivy Alvarez, Mary Kasimor, Agnes Marton, Lisa Suguitan Melnick & Eileen Tabios
Anne with an E & Me (poetry) by Wesley St. Jo
Humors (poetry) by Joel Chace
My Beauty is an Occupiable Space (poetry) by Anne Gorrick & John Bloomberg-Rissman
peminology (poetry) by Melinda Luisa de Jesús
Close Apart (poetry) by Robert Cowan
One, Two, Three: Selected Hay(na)ku Poems by Eileen R. Tabios, translated into Spanish by Rebeka Lembo (Bilingual Edition)
HAY(NA)KU 15 (poetry) edited by Eileen R. Tabios
Humanity: An Anthology edited by Eileen R. Tabios
Dictionary Volume L (poetry) by Ivy Alvarez
The Good Mother of Marseille (novel) by Christopher X. Shade
Elsewhen (poetry) by Robert Cowan
An MDR Journal by Leny M. Strobel

PALOMA PRESS
Publishing Poetry+Prose since 2016
San Mateo & Morgan Hill, CA
www.palomapress.net

With *The Great American Novel: Selected Visual Poetry (2001-2019)*, Eileen Tabios not only presents 19 years of her forays into visual poetry, but takes the reader on an extremely personal journey of exploration of cultural identity, the ramifications of colonialism, the functions of language and the possibilities of connectivity in love and pain where each poem acts as a poignant marker along the way. Each sequence in this collection vastly differs—from asemic chance operations composed of Tabios's plucked white hairs let fall into place (recalling how Duchamp composed *3 Standard Stoppages*) to a description of each poem-object in a destroyed mail art correspondence of sculpted visual poems. Tabios's openness to possibility has created poems radiating with life which are as heavy as they are celebratory. If you're looking for bubblegum, move on—here is something entirely different for your eyes to chew on.
—**Sacha Archer**, author of *Detour*

"I write in Poetry…Poetry is its own language." In the work of Eileen Tabios this sometimes means crossed-out lines, removal of substance to discover other, deeper, substance, thus unearthing the real in a sequence of forgotten things, abstractions, thoughts, people, moments . . . the recovery of each deliberately formed, reformed, performed. She lives the reality and potency of visual and textual poetry with equal fluency, melding the two, bringing us to them as she brings them to us.

Eileen Tabios is a human miracle of confident courage who invents and embraces the most difficult questions in rapid succession, and indwells in what erupts from each, demanding everything of the self within an infinity of other selves. By her being and her work, Eileen reveals that artistry at its most potent is self-aware. She embraces the stuff of life that might be art, and she erases the divide between discovery and invention.

Eileen Tabios takes part by taking apart then seaming beyond seeming. Commas as visuals take form, flight, shape. Real lines of once alive things plucked from hair inventing poetry without genuflection. Achromotricia re(de)fines asemia, emerging a new version of whiteness against cloth backdrops. Finding poetry as poetry is. Eileen asserts in natural form the joining of worlds by being knowing learning doing becoming fascinated by what creates itself around her as she fascinates us by what she makes herself.
—**Sheila E. Murphy**, author of *Reporting Live From You Know Where*

There is a close and multilayered connection between image and text in this book of Eileen Tabios' selected visual poetry projects, from 2001 to the present. In some cases we have texts within the images, as well, and more than once they come from Tabios' own verbal poetry. The images and their descriptions have a great influence on each other's effect.

I immediately got attracted to the first images, documenting an installation titled *"Pilipinz Cloudygenous"*. Then I read the notes, and went back to the images. The effect got stronger and stronger. While the mobiles of say, Fischli & Weiss, are about the funny chain of causality, Tabios' work is about a funnily represented, rather absurd, but still functioning chain—leading back to the sources. "Hanging (from a ceiling)", roots in the sky.

In *The Mortality Asemics* series, I can see—and learn from the description: the two processes are always intertwined! —how eight strands of plucked out white hair transcend into a celestial constellation and, in a parallel fashion, into the "lines" of an asemic poem. In a similar sequence, titled *The Outsider's Dilemma*, one hair falls apart from the others. It is doubly cut off from its source, and that is exactly why it, movingly, gets in the focus of the wordless poem.

The title piece is a heart-shaped red chocolate box seeming to protest through its own theatrical presence against having been dropped into a waste bin. The heart is apparently too big to be fully hidden. The work dates from 2016.

"Answers, as with the internet and diaspora, are not fixed but provided by its viewers based on their differing subjectivities." See what you read and read what you see. Tabios' wise and entertaining book reveals a multitude of contexts.

—**Márton Koppány**, author of *Endgames*

BY EILEEN R. TABIOS

POETRY
After The Egyptians Determined The Shape of the World Is A Circle, 1996
Beyond Life Sentences, 1998
The Empty Flagpole (CD with guest artist Mei-mei Berssenbrugge), 2000
Ecstatic Mutations (with short stories and essays), 2001
Reproductions of The Empty Flagpole, 2002
Enheduanna in the 21st Century, 2002
There, Where the Pages Would End, 2003
Menage a Trois With the 21st Century, 2004
Crucial Bliss Epilogues, 2004
The Estrus Gaze(s), 2005
SONGS OF THE COLON, 2005
POST BLING BLING, 2005
I Take Thee, English, For My Beloved, 2005
The Secret Lives of Punctuations, Vol. I, 2006
Dredging for Atlantis, 2006
It's Curtains, 2006
SILENCES: The Autobiography of Loss, 2007
The Singer and Others: Flamenco Hay(na)ku, 2007
The Light Sang As It Left Your Eyes: Our Autobiography, 2007
NOTA BENE EISWEIN, 2009
Footnotes to Algebra: Uncollected Poems 1995-2009, 2009
On A Pyre: An Ars Poetica, 2010
Roman Holiday, 2010
Hay(na)ku for Haiti, 2010
THE THORN ROSARY: Selected Prose Poems and New 1998-2010, 2010
the relational elations of ORPHANED ALGEBRA (with j/j hastain), 2012
5 Shades of Gray, 2012
THE AWAKENING: A Long Poem Triptych & A Poetics Fragment, 2013
147 MILLION ORPHANS (MMXI-MML), 2014
44 RESURRECTIONS, 2014
SUN STIGMATA (Sculpture Poems), 2014
I FORGOT LIGHT BURNS, 2015
DUENDE IN THE ALLEYS, 2015
INVENT(ST)ORY: SELECTED CATALOG POEMS & NEW (1996-2015), 2015
THE CONNOISSEUR OF ALLEYS, 2016
The Gilded Age of Kickstarters, 2016
Excavating the Filipino in Me, 2016
I FORGOT ARS POETICA, 2016
AMNESIA: Somebody's Memoir, 2016
THE OPPOSITE OF CLAUSTROPHOBIA: Prime's Anti-Autobiography, 2017
Post-Ecstasy Mutations, 2017

On Green Lawn, The Scent of White, 2017
TO BE AN EMPIRE IS TO BURN, 2017
If They Hadn't Worn White Hoods … (with John Bloomberg-Rissman), 2017
What Shivering Monks Comprehend, 2017
YOUR FATHER IS BALD: Selected Hay(na)ku Poems, 2017
IMMIGRANT: Hay(na)ku & Other Poems In A New Land, 2017
COMPREHENDING MORTALITY (with John Bloomberg-Rissman), 2017
Big City Cante Intermedio, 2017
WINTER ON WALL STREET: A Novella-in-Verse, 2017
MAKING NATIONAL POETRY MONTH GREAT AGAIN, 2017
MANHATTAN: An Archaeology, 2017
Love In A Time of Belligerence, 2017
MURDER DEATH RESURRECTION: A Poetry Generator (2018), 2018
HIRAETH: Tercets From The Last Archipelago, 2018
One, Two, Three: Selected Hay(na)ku Poems (Trans. Rebeka Lembo), 2018
THE GREAT AMERICAN NOVEL: Selected Visual Poetry (2001-2019), 2019
Witness in the Convex Mirror, 2019
The In(ter)vention of the Hay(na)ku: Selected Tercets (1996-2019), 2019
Drawings Form/From The Six Directions, 2019

FICTION
Behind The Blue Canvas, 2004
Novel Chatelaine, 2009
SILK EGG: Collected Novels 2009-2009, 2011

PROSE COLLECTIONS
Black Lightning: Poetry-In-Progress (poetry essays/interviews), 1998
My Romance (art essays with poems), 2002
The Blind Chatelaine's Keys (biography with haybun), 2008
AGAINST MISANTHROPY: A Life in Poetry (2015-1995), 2015
 # EileenWritesNovel, 2017

"The whole point of visual poetry, just like a traditional poem, is that the poem is presented to be read."
—Sacha Archer

CONTENTS

From "PILIPINZ CLOUDYGENOUS" (2018-2019)	11
CLOUDYGENOUS ARS POETICA (2018)	17
CLOUDYGENOUS ORIGIN (2018)	18
From "The Limits of CLOUDYGENOUS" (2018)	19
A Tree's Suicide Note (2018)	21
MY ADOPTION (2018)	23
From "EXCAVATED TANKAS" (2018)	26
From "The MDR Poetry Generator: RE-MEMBER-ING TANKA (#10)"	31
From "I Recall Forgetting A Secret From My Youth" (2018)	32
Erasing Amnesia (2018)	34
Colonial Mentality (2018)	36
Translation: Colonialism (2018)	37
Community of Vowels (2018)	41
KOMMAS: A Speculative Fiction (2016)	47
Excerpt from the Novelist's Diary (2016)	52
The Big Box Project / "Arrival: An Impossibility" (2016)	53
Mooring After Loss (2016)	55
The Great American Novel (2016)	56
"DON'T CALL ME FILIPINO" (2015)	57
For Christmas, the Hay(na)ku Visits Serbia (2015)	59
From "The Mortality Asemics (Series #3)" (2015)	60
The Outsider's Dilemma (2015)	61
The Mortality Asemics (Series #2) (2015)	63
From "The Mortality Asemics (Series #1)" (2015)	69
I Forget Forgetting My Skin Was Ruin (2015)	70
Entry (2013)	74
THE SECRET (An Unreadable Book) (2013)	75
"GIRL SINGING" (2009)	80
Poem-Sculpture Collaborations with Nick Carbo (2005)	85
Global Warming (2009)	87
Listing Poem Towards The New Filipino Society (2007)	88
The Corporate Cat (2007)	94
GRIDS (2007)	105
A Feminist Can Make Achilles Heel (2006)	112
The Secret Lives of Punctuations (2006)	113
From "Poems Form/From The Six Directions" (2001-2002)	115
Acknowledgements	123
About the Poet	127

From "PILIPINZ CLOUDYGENOUS" (2018-2019)
—a poetry and visual art installation

You leave the land of your ancestors and your birth. In the 20th and 21st centuries, you need not retain that land simply through memory. Starting last century, you can access images of and from that land through the internet. But you don't feel, when touching your computer screen, the dirt with which you once made mud with a beloved *Apong*, Grandmother, to create toys of tiny pots and plates. You don't feel, when touching your computer screen, the sweet scent of Apong's breath as she bends over your small fingers fumbling to shape a small plate. You don't feel, when touching your computer screen, her gentle kiss on your brow as she places small pieces of a ripped leaf on your plate as "dinengdeng" or Ilocano vegetable stew.

Virtual reality's images bring you closer to your birthland. But *a remove* remains and persists.

As you continue to live your life, you become more tied to life in the internet. This is true with others on the planet, whether they are in the diaspora or not. But your virtual reality life is heightened by feelings of displacement as a result of migration. As you move from one physical place to another, from one city to another and even to a rural area, you never lose the feeling of being alien—such solidifies your ties to the internet where you feel more comfortable roaming.

But *a remove* remains and persists.

For my contribution to *Counter-Desecration: A Glossary for Writing Within the Anthropocene* edited by Linda Russo and Marthe Reed (Wesleyan University Press, 2018), I created a word: "cloudygenous." As I state in *Counter-Desecration*:

> "I thought of *cloudygenous* for reflecting the contemporary integration of internet access into daily living, a practice more likely to deepen and expand in the future. Indigeneity historically is tied to the land. As human population continues to rise and becomes more dense in places, access to land may become less common, even as the internet's reach expands. Those already born and likely to be born into such an environment are likely to create a new type of culture."

> *Cloudygenous* describes the results of lifestyles and practices resulting from living in the internet so that internet becomes the "place" generating its own indigenous peoples and/or practices. This could be positive, e.g. when the internet facilitates engagement with the universe beyond one's physical borders. This could be negative, e.g. when the e-magination of the *cloudygenous* replaces physical reality and engagement with such reality. It's

not an adjective that's inherently negative or positive; it's more complicated, in the way a cloud can obscure but also generate life-supporting rain.

In the United States, Filipino-Americans have grappled with identity in a variety of ways. One way has been through language, including the birth of the terms "Filipinx" and "Pilipinx" to address issues of identity, gender, and colonialism. While I respect the thoughtful impetuses that resulted in such terms, I hesitate to apply the "x" to myself as I've not suffered in ways that others—say, transgenders—have suffered to articulate a term for themselves. I, thus, came up with "Pilipinz" as my own term for encompassing the variety of identities within "Filipino."

My project "PILIPINZ CLOUDYGENOUS" interrogates Filipino identity as affected by virtual reality. Part of my interrogation is a series of mobile sculptures. By hanging (from a ceiling), the mobiles float in space—a space that I consider a metaphor for (internet) cloud. The mobile which I present here intends to symbolize the Filipino diaspora. It hangs from a Star of David so as to reference humanity's oldest diaspora:

> "The Jews of Iraq constituted the second largest Mizrahi community in 1948 with a population of 130,000, equivalent to that of Algeria and second only to Morocco's 245,000. They are however, unequivocally the oldest diaspora community going back to the Babylonian captivity after the destruction of the Temple in 586 BCE. They can also claim to be the original Zionists, following the call of Ezra the Scribe to return to the land of their fathers in Judea.
> —from "The Iraqi Jews—The Oldest Diaspora, Now Safe in Israel" by Norman Berdichevsky, *New English Review*, February 2012)

The Star of David is also incorporated in the mobile because in the Filipino diaspora (as with other diasporas), as well as in the internet, one becomes exposed to numerous cultures and elements.

Hanging from this mobile are wooden carvings from the Philippines manufactured for the tourist trade. "Balikbayans" (the term for Filipinos returning to visit the Philippines) and other tourists often purchase such items for souvenirs. The mobile sculpture utilizes these figurines to leave them hanging in space to symbolize diasporic Filipinos. Not only are they hanging upside down but their connections to the mobile are unstable—i.e., they hang by clothespins which can easily be pinched open to let them loose and fall. The mobile structure manifests the instability and shifting nature of identity, especially in virtual reality where one can create one's persona.

"PILIPINZ CLOUDYGENOUS" is still in-progress, but is planned to be a large installation whose mixed-media ranges over mobile and other types of sculptures, drawings, photographs, and collages. The featured mobile is the first of (at least) six anticipated mobile-sculptures. A description of the six mobiles presents, I believe, the effect of cloudygenous:

> First mobile: to hang tourism-generated wood carvings
>
> Second mobile: to hang photographs of the same objects hanging in first mobile
>
> Third mobile: to hang variations or combinations of the objects hanging from the first and second mobiles
>
> Fourth mobile: to hang elements from the natural world such as leaves; a cellophane bag of dirt, pebbles or stone; tree limbs; bird feathers; fruits and flowers…
>
> Fifth mobile: to hang cotton balls masquerading as clouds
>
> Sixth mobile: to hang nothing … but emptiness

When exhibited, I can envision the mobiles hanging in a gallery against a wall that's been covered by cotton balls to evoke clouds. On the floor against the wall and beneath the mobiles would be a variety of computer devices whose screens all show clouds.

Other aspects of the installation would include photographs and drawings of images from the mobile sculptures. But aren't photographs and drawings creating objects that continue to be further *at a remove* from the "originals" of the mobile sculptures? The process and medium of and within the installation, therefore, also evoke the effect of the internet: its virtual reality may be real but contains an inherent displacement, a *remove*.

In interrogating the joint effects of the internet and diaspora, "PILIPINZ CLOUDYGENOUS" asks questions, including how best to live in the diaspora. Answers, as with the internet and diaspora, are not fixed but provided by its viewers based on their differing subjectivities.

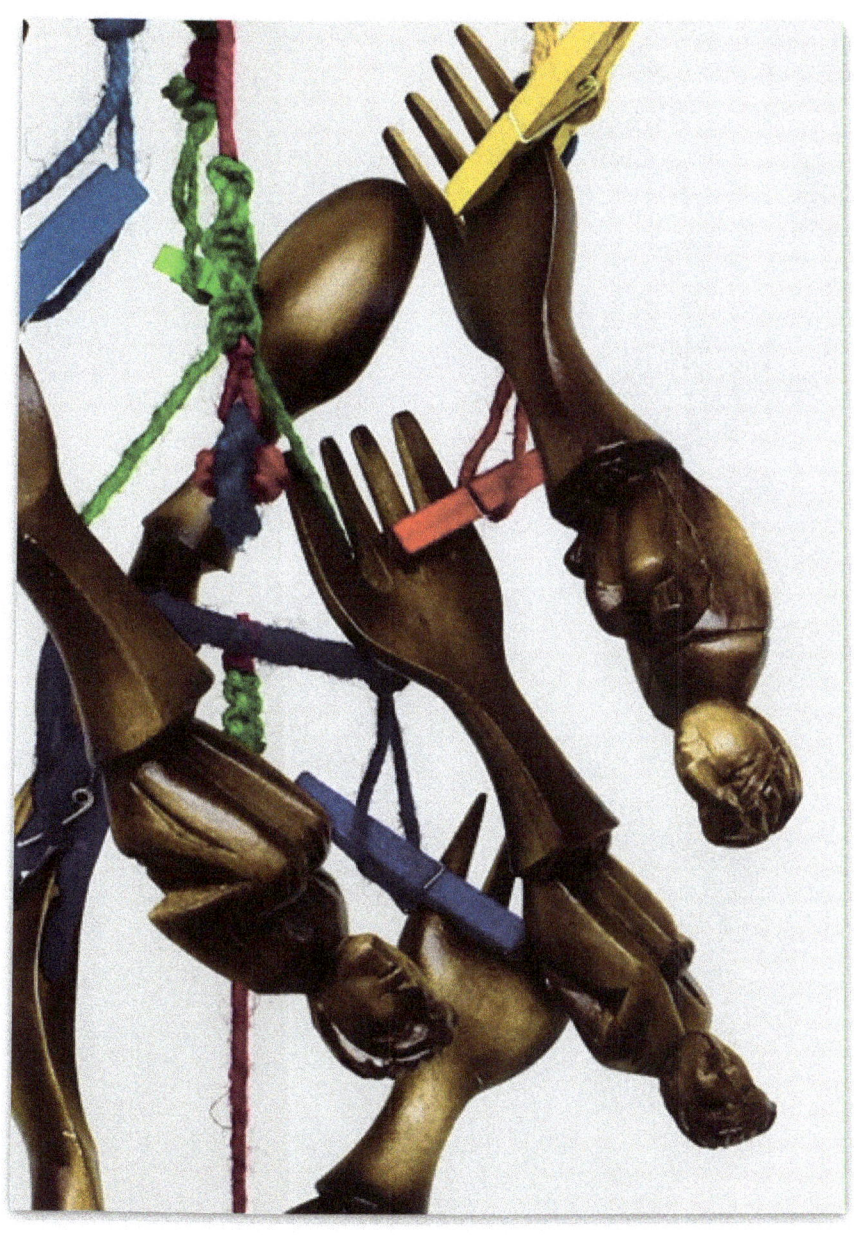

CLOUDYGENOUS ARS POETICA (2018)

I.

II.

CLOUDYGENOUS ORIGIN (2018)

A Pre-Face
Family photo in 1968, when the poet's father left the Philippines for the United States. In 1970, the rest of the family followed him.

From "The Limits of CLOUDYGENOUS" (2018)

Artist Statement

I've always loathed celebrating birthdays on Facebook. Notwithstanding the good-hearted motivations of those expressing "Happy Birthday!" to their Facebook "friends," this element is a good example of the artificiality that exists in virtual reality. "The Limits of Cloudygenous" is a series of manipulated images addressing this artifice. The sample images here present my favorite flower, roses, as well as a favorite treat, chocolate. While the images are lush, they are unsatisfactory: you can't stroke the petals or smell the perfume of roses, and you can't eat the chocolates. These failures have implications.

A Tree's Suicide Note (2018)

"I gazed in the bitter glass."

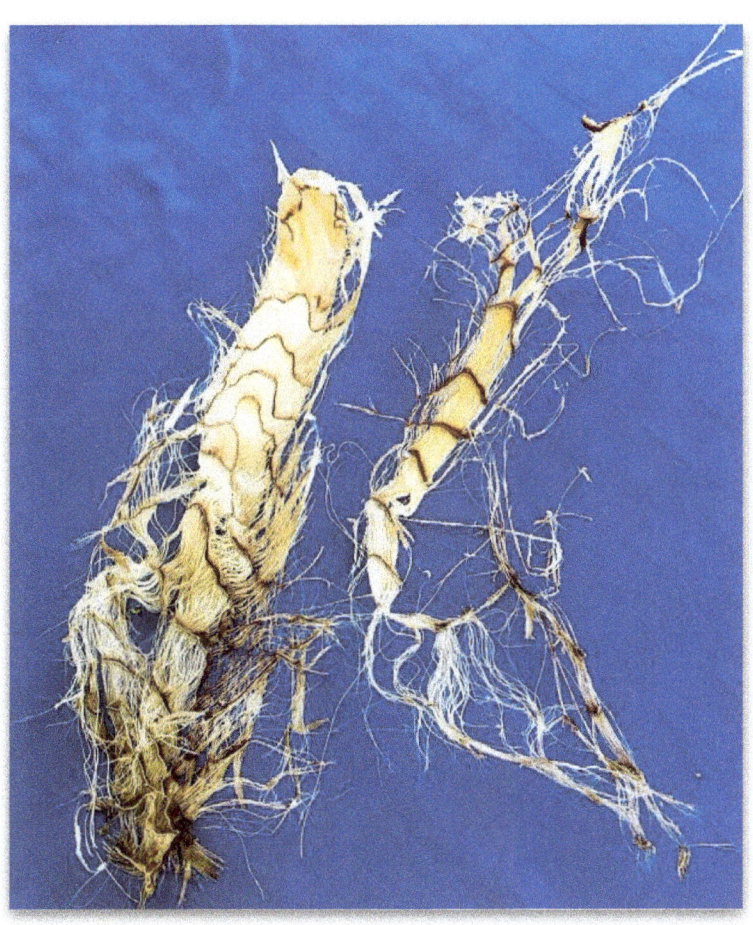

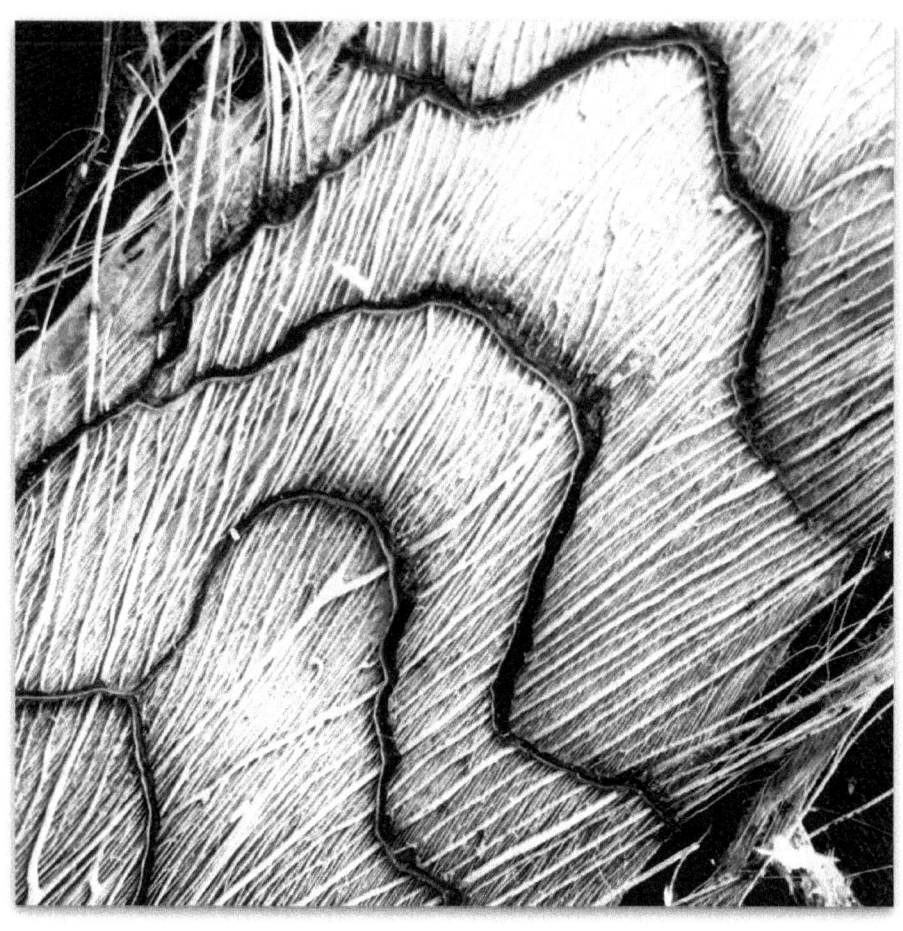

Note: Created after "Two Trees" by William Butler Yeats.

MY ADOPTION (2018)

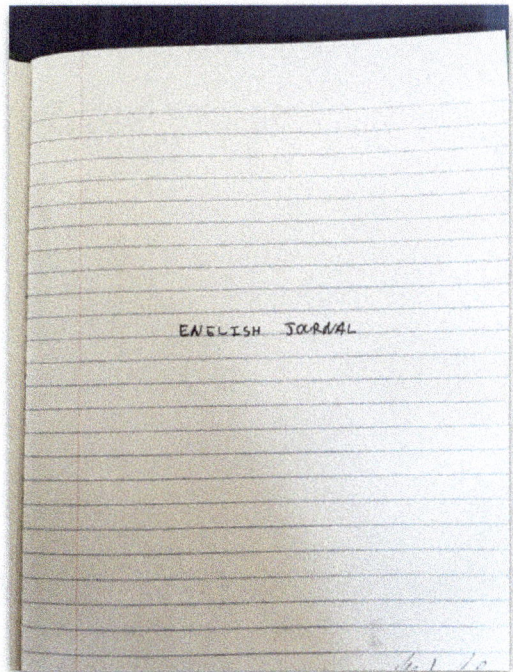

Artist Statement:

"MY ADOPTION" conflates two aspects of my adoption story. While the photographed composition notebook was owned by my real-life son who I adopted from Colombia, the series also implies something about my enforced adoption of English as a poet. The latter is referenced in this interview with John Bloomberg-Rissman first published in *ARDUITY* and most recently in the anthology *HUMANITY* (Paloma Press, San Mateo, 2018):

> In terms of behavior, where are the moments of joy, of beauty, of grace within this doomsday path humans are on? From where or how do we come up with reasons that make it worthwhile to continue living? To rush out of our beds to greet the day? To smile? To laugh? Well, for me, these moments would occur through the positive interactions made possible by love and respect for other people, creatures and the environment. Many are already behaving this way—including those working for policies curbing drastic climate changes. But they continue recycling the plastic bags, if you will, without dampening the overall rise of emissions! So if I look at these moments, and if I bear in mind my apocalyptic forecast for the human race, I view these moments—the stubbornness of their continued existence against all odds—as poetry in the sense that poetry's task is not to affirm the (unjust) status quo but to disrupt it. And so language. I write in English, you observe. But no. I write in Poetry. (It happens to be English poetry but I think the language we are addressing for purpose of our discussion is Poetry and not English.) Poetry is its own language. It can be the case that poetry, by being different from language's usual usage for communication, politics and commerce, questions if not disrupts societal norms. Such norms encompass what you call "an aesthetic regime that is at its very heart racist, misogynist, etc."
>
> Thus, my poetry language reflects having to disturb the norm which, even when generating moments of beauty, encompasses states of complacency and lack of imagination; such factors often create poor poems as well as no effective solutions for societal problems. In other venues, I've actually said that my (poetry) words attempt to transcend dictionary definitions. I also reflect the influences of abstraction and cubism to disrupt syntax. I use these and other elements (collage, found texts et al) also to reconsider the notion of "author" when each individual is bound by his/her/hir times and I rebel at these times. As a poet, I attempt not to work only within what I inherit because what's inherited is fucked up, of which my colonial history is only one facet. English was the colonizer of my birthland, the Philippines. English, but not Poetry.

From "EXCAVATED TANKAS" (2018)

Witnessed in the Convex Mirror (#27): Beyond the Stars

Something like living occurs, ~~a movement out of the dream into its codification~~ ~~like~~ **a mother's grieving transformed into** ~~a daguerreotype of~~ **a black swan** ~~perched on a boy's shoulder. But the moment's significance evaporates as the round mirror widens its circumference until the tips of its diameter melts into—you choose—pools of blood or the relieving blackness of outer space. Your choice will reveal something about you—it may not be relevant, or be the breakthrough long rumored as regards psychology~~ **Trees** ~~always~~ **fall alone in thick forests—** ~~They remind~~ *~~All has been foretold, if not told.~~* ~~Recall when Captain Kirk eagerly pointed the starship~~ *~~USS Enterprise~~* ~~towards the star archipelago—the cheesy albeit charming song observes,~~ **"Beyond the rim of the star-light:** ~~a woman." Just another romance? How often does desire for the modern lapse to the archetype?~~

<u>Tanka #148</u>

Something like living
Occurs: a mother's grief forms
A black swan's profile
When a tree falls, it's alone
Beyond the rim of star-light

Witnessed in the Convex Mirror (#16): Blind Physicists

~~In suspension,~~ **unable to advance** ~~much farther than~~ **your look intercepting mine.** ~~I was tiptoeing through a book, looking for a way to express my smile. I was contemplating the~~ **energy of a curve.** ~~I was transcending night dampness I was curing a cup of yogurt with mashed Bing cherries, thus appreciating yet again the recognition of contexts. Where we all exist,~~ **we are bound by** ~~the same~~ **gravity** ~~there is no such thing as vacuum. As it turned out, it was yogurt curing the cherries for my palate, not the other way around as the cherries were sour.~~ **Physics cannot exist without observation** ~~and, often, the blind most keenly observe~~

<u>Tanka #149</u>

    Unable to advance
    Your look intercepted mine—
    A curve quick with energy
    We are bound by gravity
    Physics exist when we see

Witnessed in the Convex Mirror (#59): Hay naku!

Photographs of friends, ~~the window and the trees~~
merging in one neutral band ~~that surrounds~~
~~a memory of you until I no longer recognize~~
~~the face, the gestures, the scent of this same~~
~~memory—so much Sturm und Drang only to end~~
~~with a beige whimper? But it's all for the best~~
~~for your body, thus mine too, to evaporate into~~
~~a song lyric. These boy bands, girl bands, trans~~
~~bands emote so well into microphones. Plus their~~
~~dances! Plus their outfits! So many sequins!~~
~~There could be a worse ending to romance—~~
~~I know~~ **you,** ~~too, are~~ **sitting by a window watching**
~~yourself watching~~ **the moon slip away into haiku**

    <u>Tanka #150</u>

    Photographs of friends
    Merge into one neutral band
    Who recognizes
    ~~You~~ Who, lingering by windows
    Watching moons fall to haiku

Witnessed in the Convex Mirror (#23): Not A Pen

~~To yield what are~~ **laws of perspective**
~~as if the impact of perfume~~
                              ~~against a raised wrist~~
~~can be rehearsed. She wanted to evoke~~
~~danger and thought she found its metaphor~~
~~in cinnabar. But the flesh was too red—~~
~~she forgot~~ **anticipation begets heat.** ~~After~~
~~the scent sprawled on her skin, the result~~
~~was not the enticement of risk but~~
~~the end of winter. She paused her pen~~
~~to consider what was just written upon~~
~~a piece of white birch delivered to her~~
~~in an envelope that, when opened, released~~
~~a stallion of musk. *I failed*, she thought as~~
~~she considered the raw page whose perfume~~
~~bore an intensity she'd wanted to match~~
~~with words. But what cannot be rehearsed~~
~~cannot be measured. What is reflected~~
~~in a convex mirror presents no reasonable~~
~~extrapolation of what might surface on glass~~
~~bent to pulsate forth as convex. It is not~~
~~natural for glass to bend. Why judge a thing~~
~~when it's been forced out of its nature?~~
~~The same question for a *someone*.~~ **How
can words against bark elicit the image of
a horse nuzzling it away from its birthland tree?**
~~Had she maintained perspective, she would~~
~~have understood: to desire inevitably is to set~~
~~upon the dried bark, not a pen but, a match~~

Tanka #159

    Laws of perspective
    Often melt before the heat
    Of anticipa-
          tion: how else can words etched on
    bark reveal your looming horse?

Witnessed in the Convex Mirror: Tense Past Tense

~~The~~ **gray glaze of the past** ~~attacks all know-how:~~

~~He taught you how a "kiss" can be defined~~
~~so expansively its meaning can encompass a bite~~
~~so keen it split a lip's membrane~~
~~to release blood whose taste you had never known~~
~~could be so exquisite~~
~~it shall become a memory that shall surface for years~~
~~without your bidding and whose presence~~
~~shall make itself known through your teeth baring themselves at air~~
~~You don't write poems like he does~~
~~but you sing your dirges loudly because~~
~~his poems invited you to reconfigure~~
~~what your eyes fear but have no choice in seeing—~~
how an empty street becomes a long knife
~~a clown's face becomes the~~ *threshold to a nightmare*
~~a cluster of~~ *bees become soldiers battling the Nazis*
~~your father's senility becomes an open door for reconciliation~~
the fog spilling over a hill forms a day's source of grace
~~the sky becomes an eggshell easily punctured by turkey vultures—~~
~~he gave you an unwrapped gift~~
~~you once thought you could never repay~~

Tanka #160

    Gray glaze of the past—
    How an empty street becomes
    A knife, then threshold
    To a nightmare of mad bees
    Fog forms a day's source of grace

From "The MDR Poetry Generator" (2018)

RE-MEMBER-ING TANKA (#10)

~~58: I will always remember how, as I felt the~~ **rumble of a train** ~~arriving and departing, I stood in anticipation of the approaching world you would bring.~~

~~59: I forgot the grandfather who willingly faced a fire,~~ **fist** ~~trembling~~ **at** ~~the~~ **indifferent sky.**

~~60: I forgot the grandfather who stood before the~~ **fire** ~~rushing through~~ **a legacy** ~~untouched by 300 years of Spanish colonialism.~~

~~61:~~ **I forgot** ~~the~~ **elders,** ~~shoulders sagged to ruin, dropping gazes like debris~~ **and** ~~treasuring~~ **trees** ~~for their shade that exacts no price.~~

~~62: I forgot a country~~ **somewhere,** ~~always at the opposite of where~~ **I stand on this earth.**

Rumble of a train
Fist at indifferent sky
Fire a legacy
I forgot elders and trees
Somewhere, I stand on this earth

From "I Recall Forgetting A Secret From My Youth" (2018)

148: *I forgot you wanted to see her seeing herself…*

149: I forgot you thought of me as you paced the streets of a city whose sidewalks memorized the music of my footsteps dancing away from youth into courage.

148: *I forgot you wanted to see her seeing herself…*

149: I forgot you thought of me as you paced the streets of a city whose sidewalks memorized the music of my footsteps dancing away from youth into courage.

Erasing Amnesia (2018)

464: I forgot the delicate scrim of fine wrinkles.

465: I forgot omission as confession.

466: I forgot moonlight revealing itself as broken.

467: I forgot the noiseless convulsion.

468: I forgot the deception of diamonds.

469: I forgot the audacity of cruelty.

470: I forgot a caravan of sad hags.

471: I forgot ivory.

472: I forgot a sea refusing to swallow gold coins despite their flirtatious glints.

473: I forgot something is nullified when butter melts.

474: I forgot even false witches salsa.

475: I forgot the chef who lacked insurance.

476: I forgot stitching together a map and fur-covered boots.

477: I forgot dungeons waste marble.

478: I forgot regret is a Kingdom with unknown borders.

479: I forgot forgiveness need not be a brass coin.

480: I forgot the awkward blanket of trust.

~~...~~ delicate scrim of fine wrinkles.

~~...~~

~~...~~ moonlight revealing itself as broken.

~~...~~

~~...~~ deception of diamonds.

~~...~~

~~...~~ caravan of sad hags.

~~...~~

~~...~~ sea refusing ~~...~~ gold coins ~~...~~

~~...~~

~~...~~ false witches ~~...~~

~~...~~

~~...~~ stitching together a map ~~...~~

~~...~~

~~...~~ regret ~~is~~ a Kingdom ~~...~~

~~...~~

~~...~~ awkward blanket of trust.

Colonial Mentality (2018)

"colonial mentality is characterized by automatic preference for anything American"
—from "Activation and Automaticity of Colonial Mentality" by E.J.R. David and Sumie Okazaki

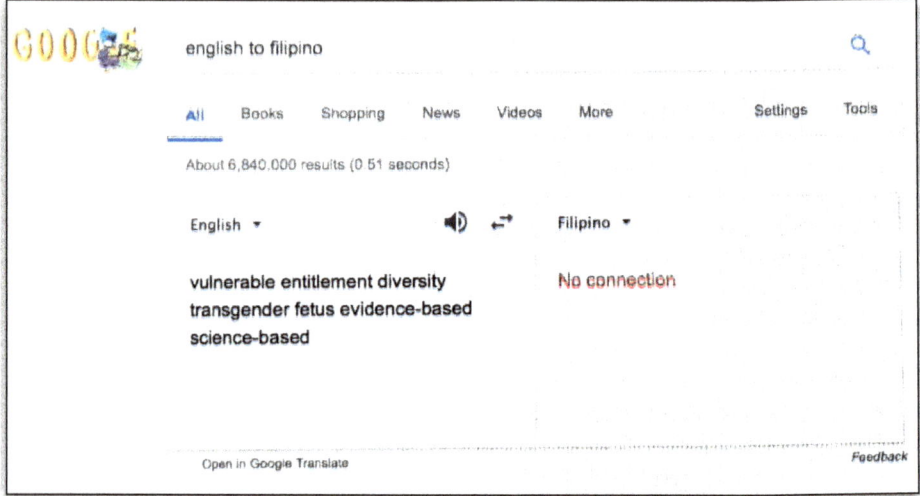

Translation: Colonialism (2018)

In mid-December 2017, media coverage revealed how, in U.S. President Trump's Administration, officials at The Centers for Disease Control (CDC), the nation's top public health agency, are discouraged from using seven words or phrases:

> vulnerable
> entitlement
> diversity
> transgender
> fetus
> evidence-based
> science-based

While first reported as a "ban," the matter was subsequently fleshed out to be one of gauging the political temper of the times and CDC staff then concluding that these words would be best avoided in order to garner Administration support for its various (proposed) programs. Such conclusion is not as sexy headline-making as "ban" but probably a more nuanced assessment of the Administration's inclinations.

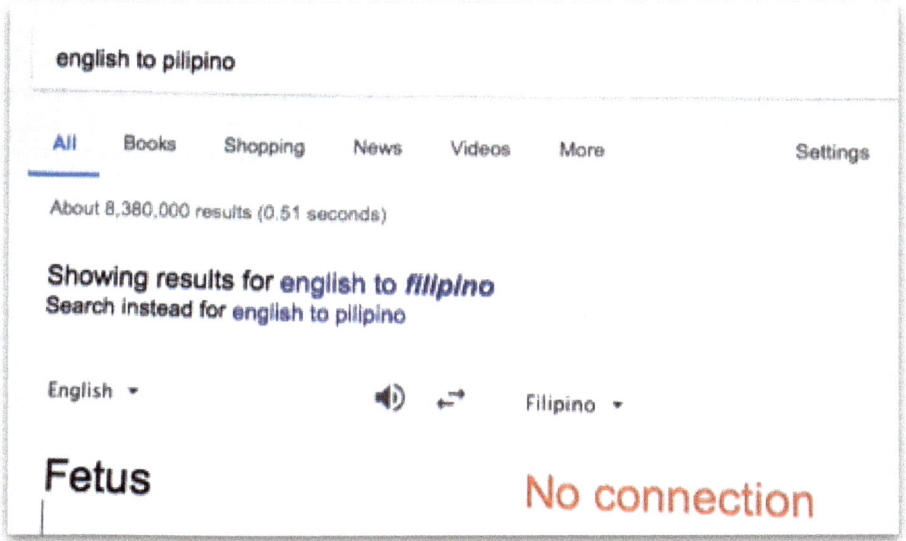

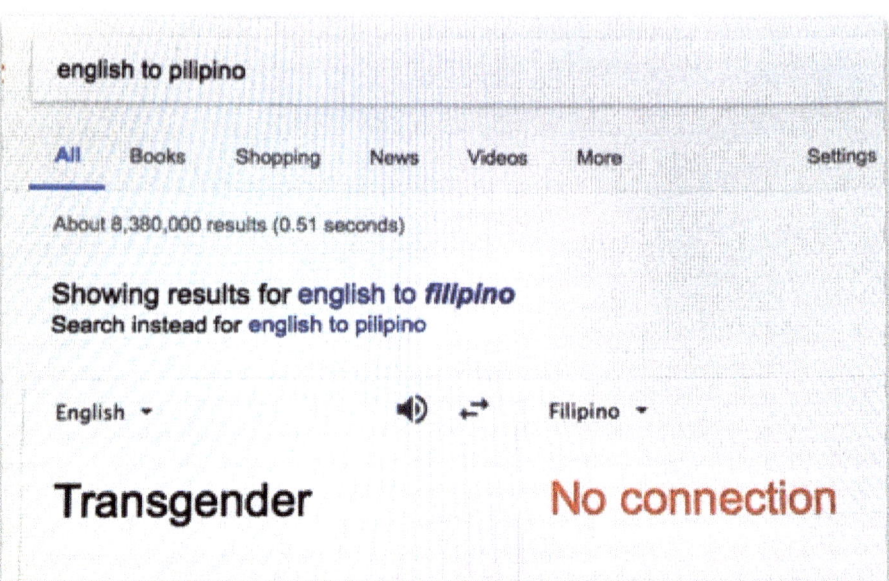

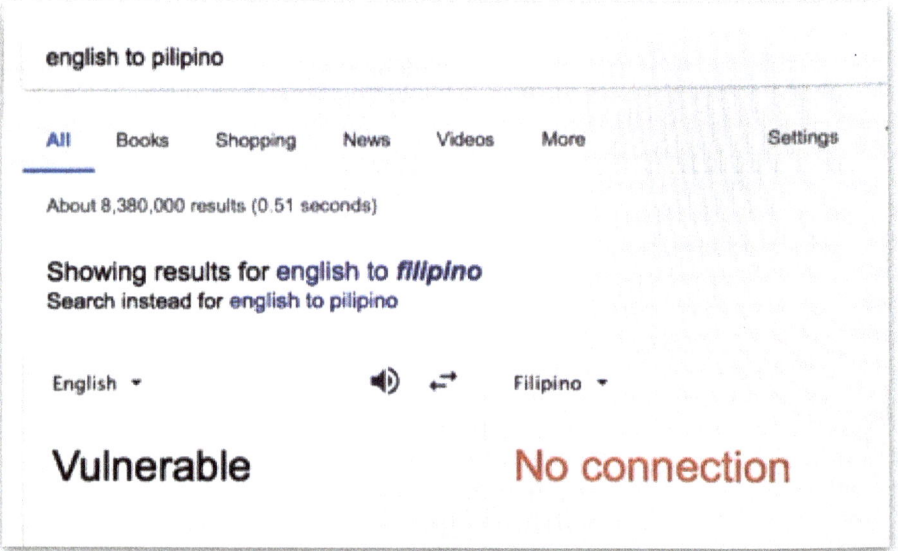

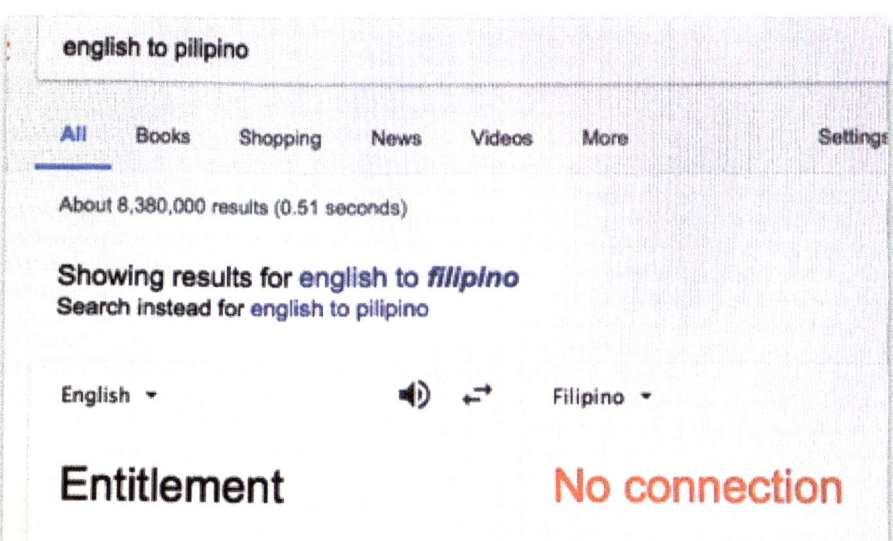
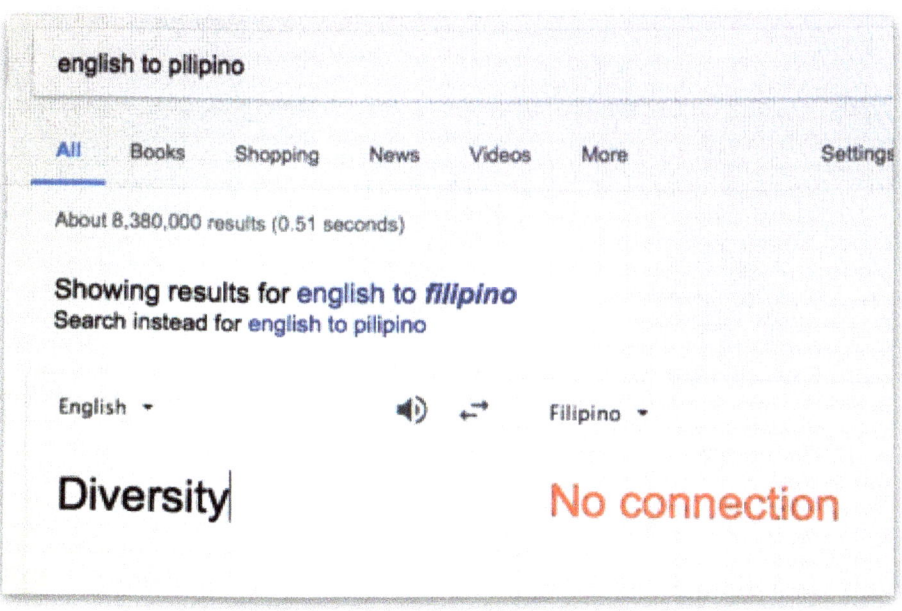

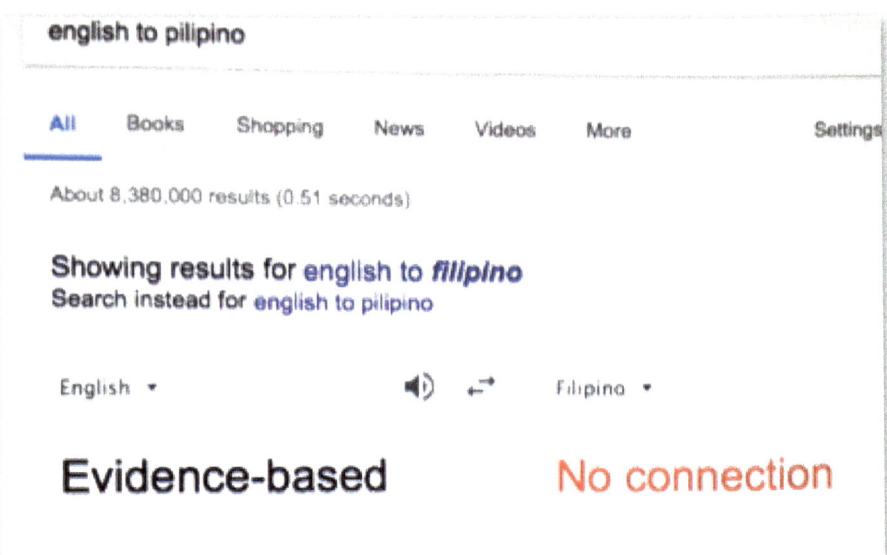

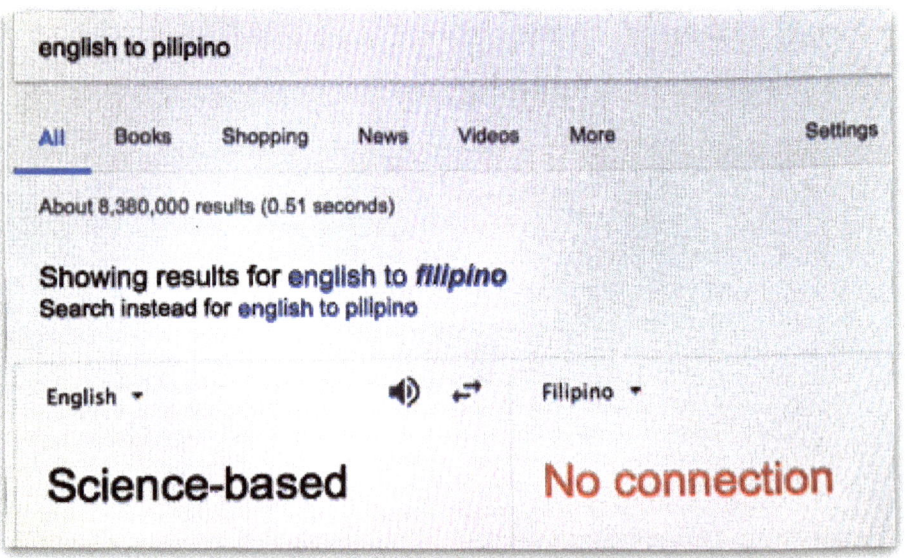

Community of Vowels (2018)

Artist Statement:
"I'm conflicted with the term "community." Many give it positive lip-service; I do, too. But community often fails/fragments/etc. — not to mention, irritates — in real life. So I wanted to pause and allow a visual metaphor for when community works. I trust that other viewers would agree with me that the images of more than one or all of the vowels in the English language create a more pleasing visual image than the (first) one-vowel image of Grid A. Vowels were connected together from a randomly-chosen page of my MDR Poetry Generator project (https://eileenrtabios.com/projects/the-mdr-poetry-generator/). Vowels were chosen for being pro-Song. Note also that the more that one vowel is involved, the more obscured is the underlying text—with such, I hoped to indicate less didactic talking at each other and more in-unison or in-harmony singing. So, let us sing together, you and I …"

GRID A

31: I forgot my hope he would speak of me to his friend who became a stranger after so many neighborly greetings in elevator rides from a past we shared before a certain diagnosis: "HIV-Positive."

32: I forgot my hope he would speak of the neighbor who understood each gift is unique and cannot be replicated away from context.

33: I also forgot foraging in a supermarket's "Sales!" bin. I forgot the three coconuts I recovered from the depths of the box which might have become their coffin. I forgot that I knew: within their hairy, brown and mottled shells, their meat would be sweet and water pure.

34: I forgot moths as the sun disappeared—"the flutter of wings as they teased a dim porch light."

35: I forgot how the faces of elders bestow a haunting on others reciprocating with their own weariness.

36: I forgot how gazes can drop like debris.

37: I forgot missing teeth and gums full of potholes.

38: I forgot how shoulders sagged to crumbling ruins as they sat by roadsides under trees whose shade they treasured for costing nothing.

39: I forgot the young hugging the ground, their damp faces eagerly turning here, eagerly turning there, searching their surroundings for treasures invisible but I also believed existed when I still shared their innocence.

40: I forgot there is a country somewhere on the opposite of where I stand on this earth, a country whose scents stubbornly perfume my dreams.

41: I forgot my mistake. The radically old and the radically young are the same in their difference from me—they do not need much, they need too much. They do not ask, they must often plead. I forgot how, unlike them, I knew what it took to survive.

42: I forgot that survival meant to move on from where a man and a woman joined before the onset of weakness to create me.

43: I forgot that to return bore no relationship to survival, which instead related to you whose path crossed mine in a new land.

44: I forgot a country somewhere was dying without a protest from me defensively—selfishly—seeking rebirth in your arms.

GRID A E

31: I forgot my hope he would speak of me to his friend who became a stranger after so many neighborly greetings in elevator rides from a past we shared before a certain diagnosis: "HIV-Positive."

32: I forgot my hope he would speak of the neighbor who understood each gift is unique and cannot be replicated away from context.

33: I also forgot foraging in a supermarket's "Sale!" bin. I forgot the three coconuts I recovered from the depths of the box which might have become their coffin. I forgot that I knew, within their hairy, brown and mottled shells, their meat would be sweet and water pure.

34: I forgot moths as the sun disappeared—"the flutter of wings as they teased a dim porch light."

35: I forgot how the faces of elders bestow a haunting on others reciprocating with their own weariness.

36: I forgot how gazes can drop like debris.

37: I forgot missing teeth and gums full of potholes.

38: I forgot how shoulders sagged to crumbling ruins as they sat by roadsides under trees whose shade they treasured for costing nothing.

39: I forgot the young hugging the ground, their damp faces eagerly turning here, eagerly turning there, searching their surroundings for treasures invisible but I also believed existed when I still shared their innocence.

40: I forgot there is a country somewhere on the opposite of where I stand on this earth, a country whose scents stubbornly perfume my dreams.

41: I forgot my mistake. The radically old and the radically young are the same in their difference from me—they do not need much, they need too much. They do not ask, they must often plead. I forgot how, unlike them, I know what it took to survive. • • •

42: I forgot that survival meant to move on from where a man and a woman joined before the onset of weakness to create me.

43: I forgot that to return bore no relationship to survival, which instead related to you whose path crossed mine in a new land.

44: I forgot a country somewhere was dying without a protest from me defensively—selfishly—seeking rebirth in your arms. • • •

GRID A E I

31: I forgot my hope he would speak of me to his friend who became a stranger after so many neighborly greetings in elevator rides from a past we shared before a certain diagnosis: "HIV-Positive."

32: I forgot my hope he would speak of the neighbor who understood each gift is unique and cannot be replicated away from context.

33: I also forgot foraging in a supermarket's "Select" bin. I forgot the three coconuts I recovered from the depths of the box which might have become their coffin. I forgot that I knew: within their hairy, brown and mottled shells, their meat would be sweet and water pure.

34: I forgot moths as the sun disappeared—"the flutter of wings as they teased a dim porch light."

35: I forgot how the faces of elders bestow a haunting on others reciprocating with their own weariness.

36: I forgot how gazes can drop like debris.

37: I forgot missing teeth and gums full of potholes.

38: I forgot how shoulders sagged to crumbling ruins as they sat by roadsides under trees whose shade they treasured for costing nothing.

39: I forgot the young hugging the ground, their damp faces eagerly turning here, eagerly turning there, searching their surroundings for treasures invisible but I also believed existed when I still shared their innocence.

40: I forgot there is a country somewhere on the opposite of where I stand on this earth, a country whose scents stubbornly perfume my dreams.

41: I forgot my mistake. The radically old and the radically young are the same in their difference from me—they do not need much, they need too much. They do not ask, they must often plead. I forgot how, unlike them, I knew what it took to survive.

42: I forgot that survival meant to move on from where a man and a woman joined before the onset of weakness to create me.

43: I forgot that to return bore no relationship to survival, which instead related to you whose path crossed mine in a new land.

44: I forgot a country somewhere was dying without a protest from me defensively—selfishly—seeking rebirth in your arms.

GRID A E I O

31: I forgot my hope he would speak of me to his friend who became a stranger after staying my neighbor, my greetings in stuttering notes from a past we shared before a certain diagnosis: "HIV-Positive."

32: I forgot my hope he would speak of the neighbor who understood each gift is unique and cannot be replicated away from context.

33: I also forgot foraging in a supermarket's "Sales!" bin. I forgot the three coconuts I recovered from the depths of the box which might have become their coffin. I forgot that I knew, within their hairy, brown and mottled shells, their meat would be sweet and water pure.

34: I forgot moans as the sun disappeared—"the flutter of wings as they teased a dim patch light."

35: I forgot how the faces of elders bestow a haunting on others reciprocating with their own weariness.

36: I forgot how gazes can drop like debris.

37: I forgot missing teeth and gums full of pinholes.

38: I forgot how shoulders sagged to crumbling ruins as they sat by roadsides under trees whose shade they treasured for costing nothing.

39: I forgot the young hugging the ground, their damp faces eagerly turning here, eagerly turning there, searching their surroundings for treasures invisible but I also believed existed when I still shared their innocence.

40: I forgot there is a country somewhere on the opposite of where I stand on this earth, a country whose scents stubbornly perfume my dreams.

41: I forgot my mistake. The radically old and the radically young are the same in their difference from me—they do not need much, they need so much. They do not ask, they must often plead. I forgot how, unlike them, I know what it took to survive. * * * *

42: I forgot that survival meant to move on from where a man and a woman joined before the onset of weakness to create me.

43: I forgot that to return bore no relationship to survival, which instead related to you whose path crossed mine in a new land.

44: I forgot a country somewhere was dying without a protest from me — thieving — selfishly — seeking rebirth in your arms. * * * *

45

GRID A E I O U

31: I forgot my hope he would speak of me to his friend who became a stranger after so many neighborly greetings in seeing a note from a past we shared before a certain diagnosis: "HIV-Positive."

32: I forgot my hope he would sustain the neighbor who understood each gift is unique and cannot be replicated away from context.

33: I also forgot seeing in a supermarket's "Sales" bin, I forgot the three coconuts I rescued from the depths of the box which might have become their coffin. I forgot that I knew, within their hairy, brown and matted shells, their meat would be sweet and water pure.

34: I forgot moths as the sun disappeared—"the flutter of wings as they teased a dim porch light."

35: I forgot how the faces of elders bestow a haunting on others reciprocating with their own weariness.

36: I forgot how gazes can drop like debris.

37: I forgot missing teeth and gums full of potholes.

38: I forgot how shoulders sagged to crumbling ruins as they sat by roadsides under trees whose shade they treasured for costing nothing.

39: I forgot the young hugging the ground, their dusty faces eagerly turning here, eagerly turning there, searching their surroundings for treasures invisible but I also believed existed when I still shared their innocence.

40: I forgot there is a country somewhere on the opposite of where I stand on this earth, a country whose scents stubbornly perfume my dreams.

41: I forgot my mistake. The radically old and the radically young are the same in their difference from me—they do not ask much, they need as much. They do not ask, they must often plead. I forgot how, unlike them, I knew what it took to survive.

42: I forgot that survival meant to move on from where a man and a woman joined before the onset of weakness to create me.

43: I forgot that to return bore no relationship to survival, which instead related to you whose path crossed mine in a new land.

44: I forgot a country somewhere was dying without a protest from me defensively—selfishly—seeking rebirth in your arms.

KOMMAS: A Speculative Fiction (2016)

Kommas Fall From the Mother Ship

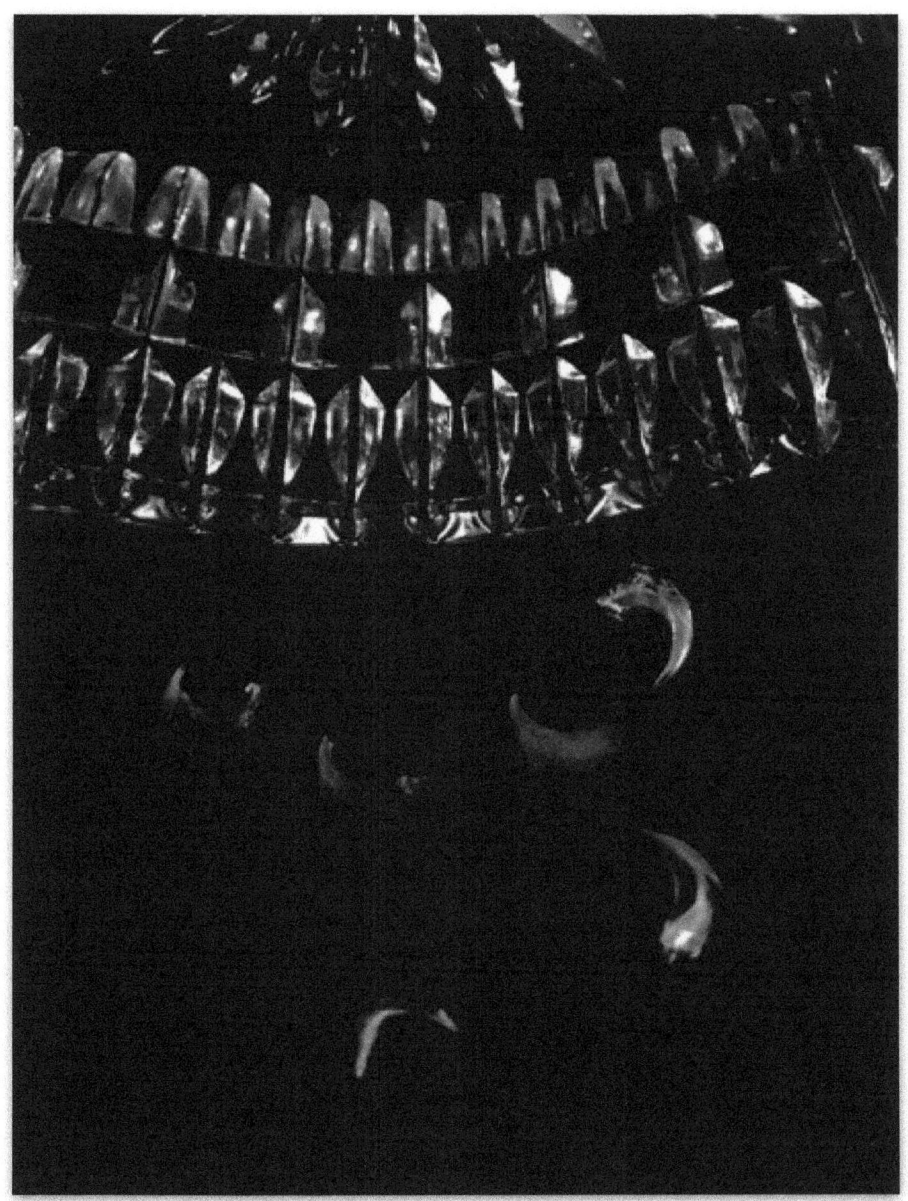

Kommas Konsider Arkitekture

Komma-Klawed Magnolia

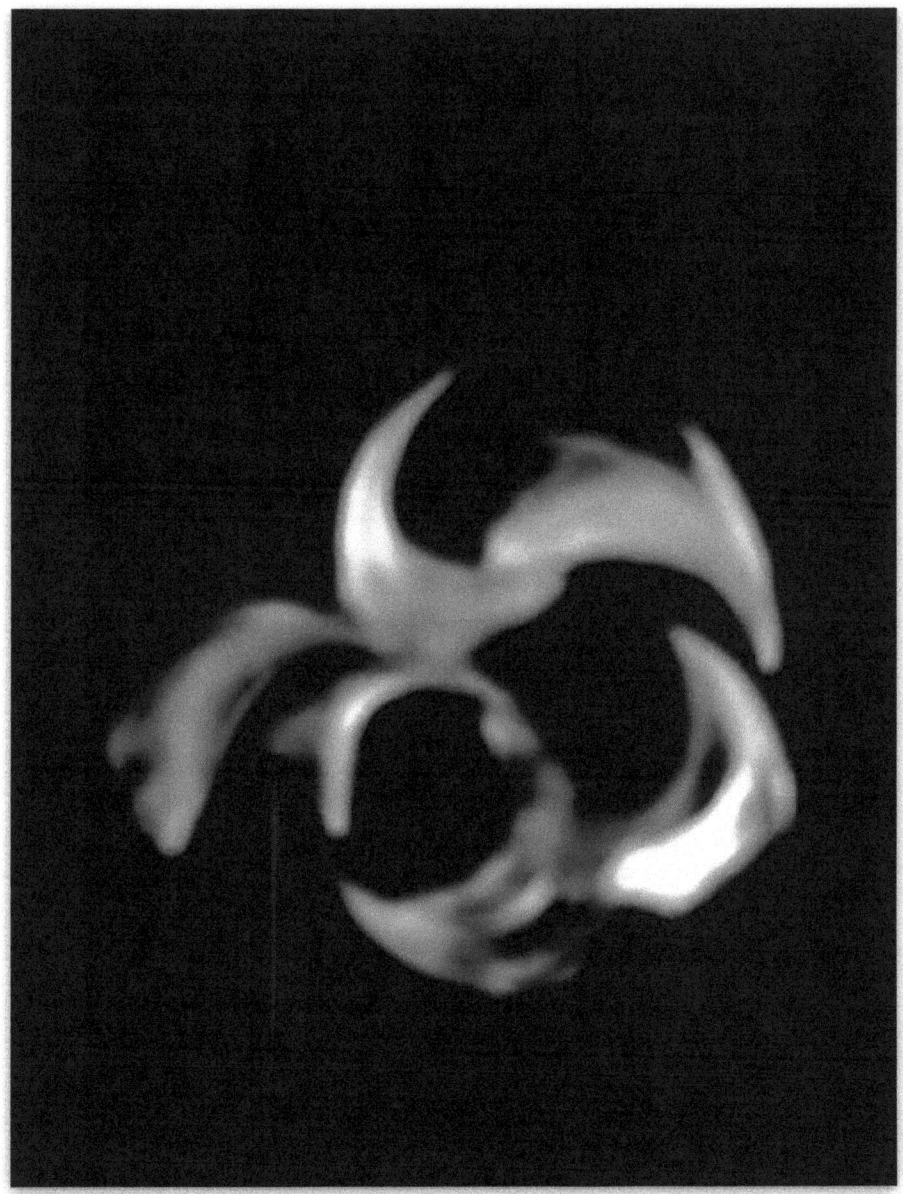

False Kloud Over Komma

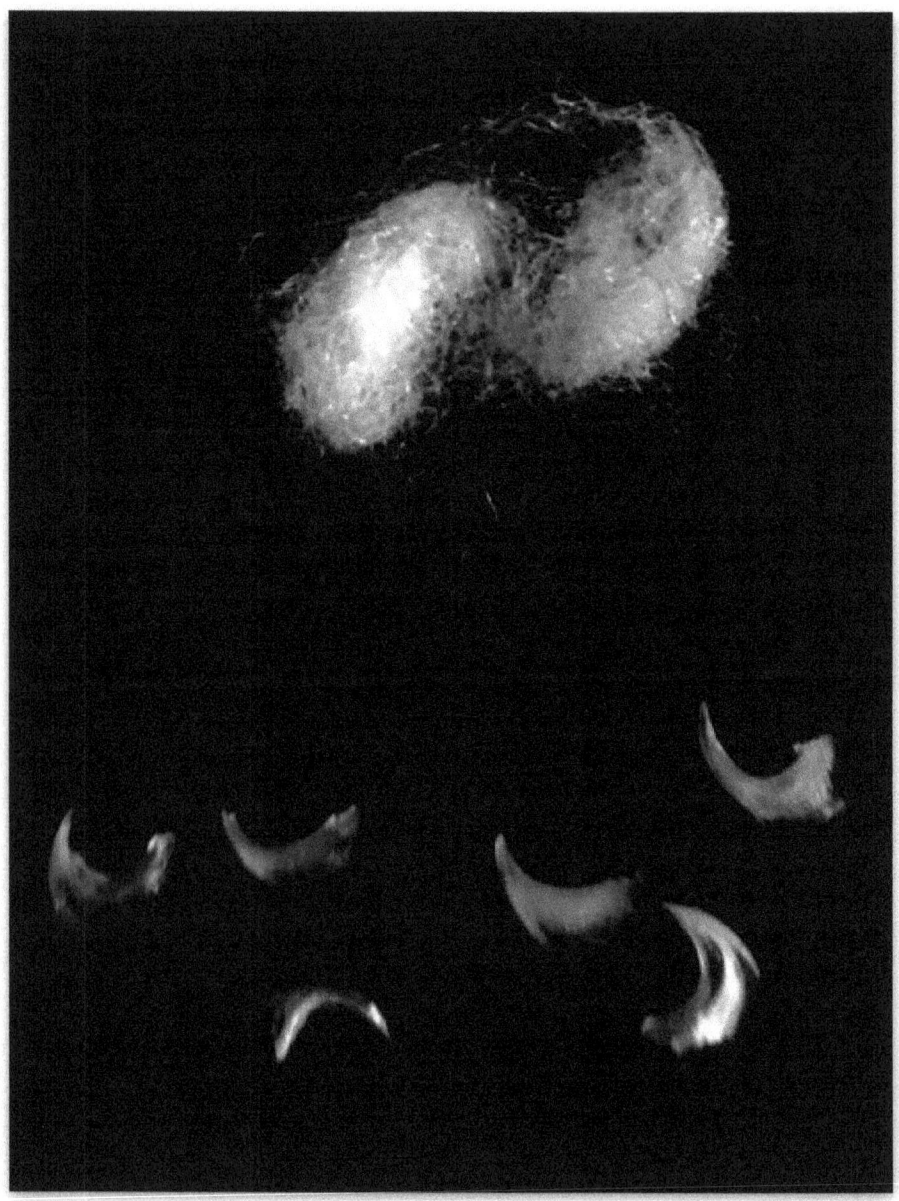

Komma Mandala

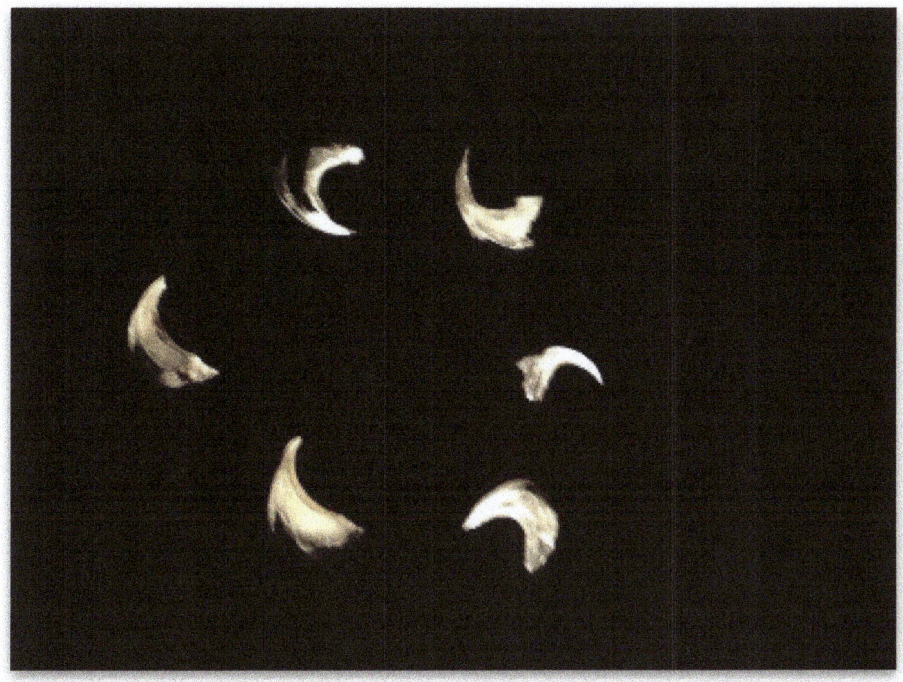

Media: ~~Cat claws~~ Kat klaws, cotton ball, crystal bowl, black-painted wood.

Excerpt from the Novelist's Diary (2016)

The Big Box Project / "Arrival: An Impossibility" (2016)

Curator of "The Big Box Poetry Project," Pamela Hart placed poems on big box stores and related venues—Starbucks, sidewalks, airports, etc. I'm delighted that my poem "Arrival: An Impossibility" was a participant—it was taped over a "No Trespassing" sign by a Walgreens!

The poem on the trespassing print-out is a verse poem; what makes it visual is how it trespassed to subvert a Big Box Store's space—architectural visual poetry!

Nonetheless, here's the text poem (in an updated version):

ARRIVAL: AN IMPOSSIBILITY

As I recall, it itched

"Dirty-white" can be the euphemism
        for its uncertain color

But all the aunties wanted its symbol
that *Someone has arrived!*

In the old country, arrival in the colonizer's house sufficed

In the new country, immigrants learned
much work and more luck was required

Those who have truly arrived can
afford a fur coat, and so the aunties quarreled
for that particular inheritance

Their words irritated my father
the only son, thus, only heir
He chose to bury his mother in her fur
cape with a single button of mother-of-pearl

Dad's only daughter, I was asked
if I objected as other relatives thought
I, as female, should be the garment's rightful heir

I said I was happy with Dad's decision—
I knew the fur to be as fake
as the idea one can ever arrive
to everybody's satisfaction

or the idea another destination
should be privileged
over the land which willingly heard
one's infantile screams against arriving
into a cruel cruel world …

Mooring After Loss (2016)

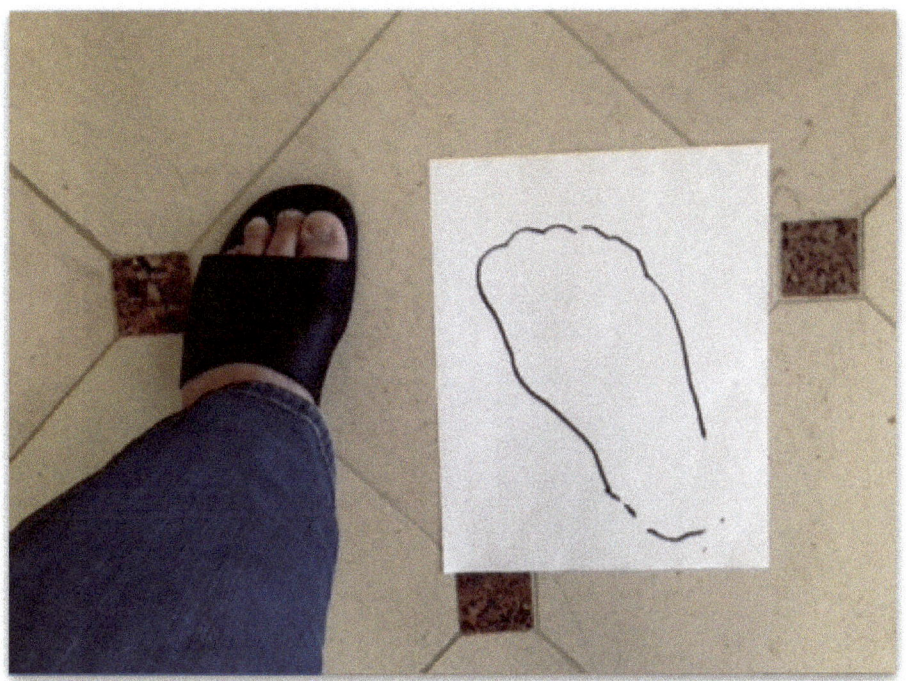

The Great American Novel (2016)

DON'T CALL ME "FILIPINO" (2015)

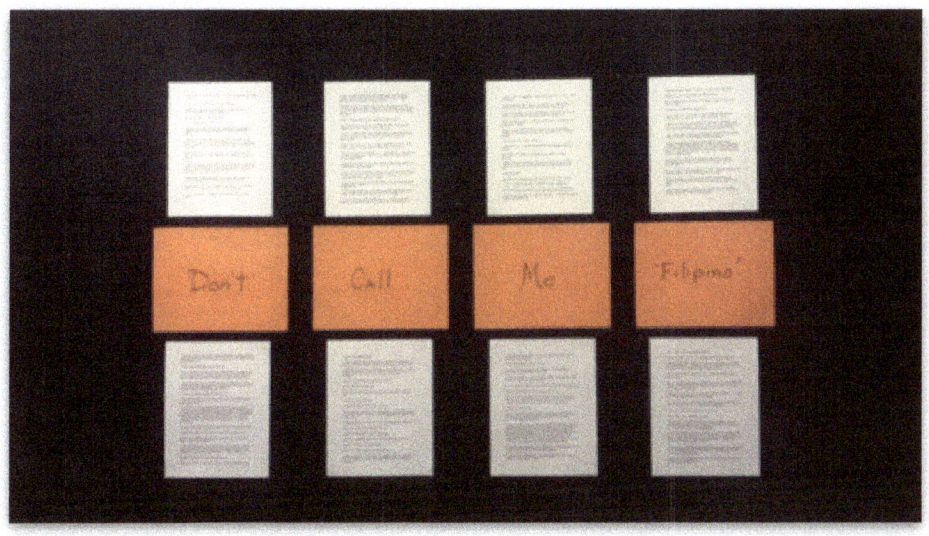

Photographs by Alfred Yuson

"DON'T CALL ME 'FILIPINO'" was discussed in *Excavating the Filipino In Me* (Tinfish, Hawai'i, 2016), e.g. this excerpt from the interview by Pearl Yasmin:

> **Pearl Yasmin:** I also see some major biographical disruption in your two poems "DON'T" and "Excavating the Filipino in Me."
>
> **Eileen Tabios:** Last year I guest-edited a theme issue on the List or Catalog Poem for the literary journal *TRUCK*. One of the contributors, lars palm, had a poem "(approximate play list new years eve 2014/15)" that included the line and reference to punk rock band NOFX's "dont call me white." I found it on YouTube and played it (am playing it as I write this). The YouTube commentary also included someone who lauded its message as a demand not to be categorized (as "white") but to be perceived as an individual.
>
> While this demand, or suggestion, would not seem unreasonable, it is a position that obviously is different when made by a white person versus a person of color (POC) (different partly due to issues of "white privilege"). I was interested in exploring the difference between a white person and a POC making that demand.
>
> Thus, I created the visual poem "Don't Call Me 'Filipino'." One thing different about POC is the notion of authenticity—from insults like a black person being called an "Oreo cookie" (black on the outside but white inside) to a POC writer's work being deemed inauthentic and/ or whitewashed if it doesn't adequately address origin and race. Thus, for me to release a work positing publicly, "Don't Call Me 'Filipino'" would not just be—as in NOFX's case—a demand not to be categorized but also lay open the POC author—me—to charges of racial self-hatred and (for a Filipino) colonial mentality.
>
> Yet I also felt, looking at the four-page visual poem, that as a POC my demand to not be categorized but be considered individually has more strength than a white person's demand for not being called white—an effectiveness made possible paradoxically by the POC person's past experiencing of racism and colonialism. In this sense, I was initially pleased by this poem as I thought the invisible postscript to this work could be a page with the line, "Call me 'Eileen R. Tabios'."

For Christmas, the Hay(na)ku Visits Serbia (2015)

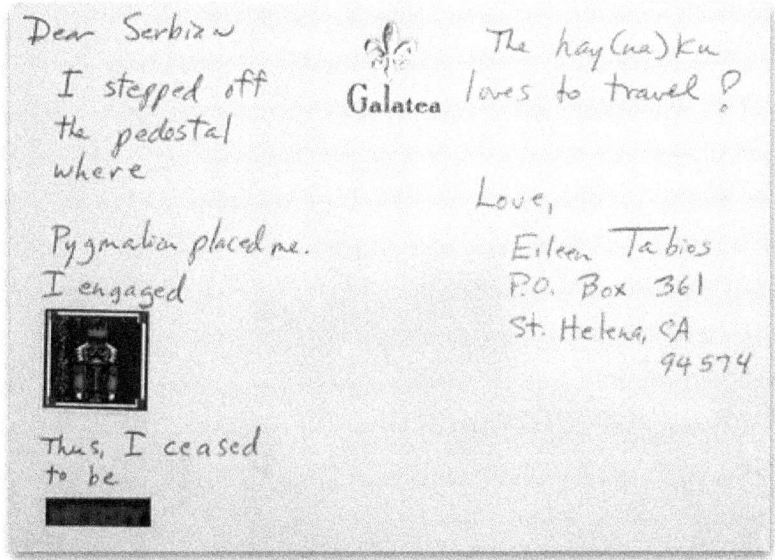

Artist Notes:
Recycled Xmas stickers and stationery referencing Galatea—thus, also Pygmalion—become a postcard for a Mail Art exhibit in Serbia curated by Dejan Bogojevic.

The hay(na)ku postcard poem-text is

> Dear Serbia,
>
> I stepped off
> the pedestal
> where
>
> Pygmalion placed me.
> I engaged
> [XMAS STICKER OF TOY SOLDIER]
>
> Thus, I ceased
> to be
> MERRY

The last word is another Xmas sticker proclaiming the word "MERRY". Here, we have the ubiquitous image of a Christmas toy soldier becoming the metaphor for the misogynist man (Pygmalion). I could go on, but hey, I'd rather enjoy the holidays ...

December 2015

From "The Mortality Asemics (Series #3)" (2015)

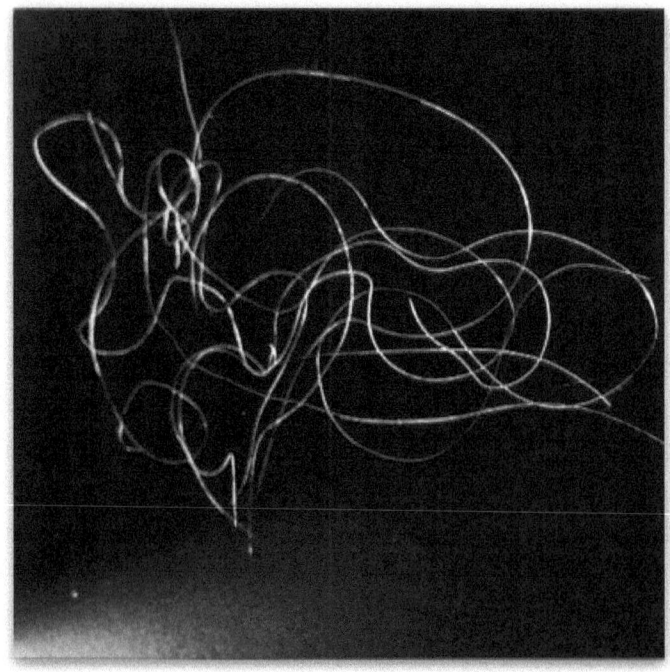

The Outsider's Dilemma (2015)

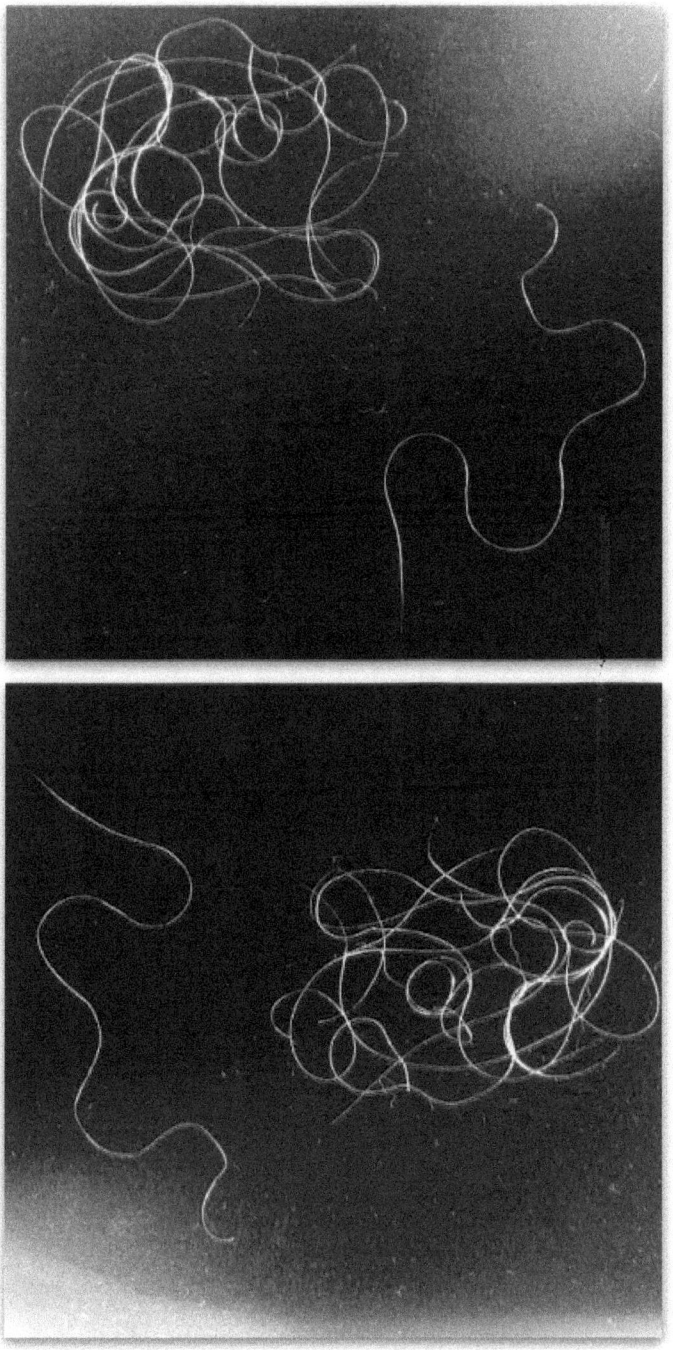

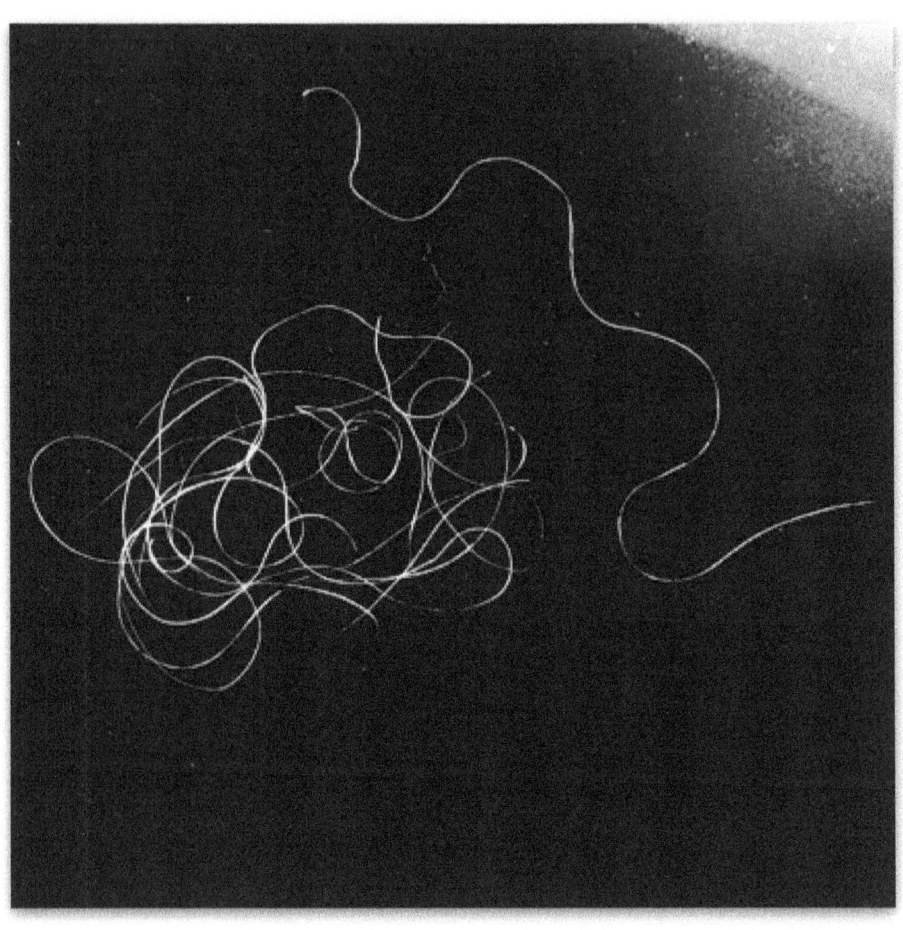

The Mortality Asemics (Series #2) (2015)

"Achromotricia" is a word I learned in order to write about ... achromotricia, the loss of hair color. As a word it doesn't roll easily on the tongue. It shouldn't. While achromotricia is usually associated with age, my experience of it is one of ~~experiencing~~ suffering radical stress, the type of pressure that whitens Presidents' hairs.

My hair started whitening about five years ago. For privacy reasons, I can't go into the root (pun intended) source of the pressure that introduced snow to my naturally black hair. I will just fast forward to my conclusion about my white hair: it's not something I accept as part of aging gracefully or graciously; simply, I find these achromotriciaed (it's a word because I'm a poet and made it so) hair loathsome because of their underlying stressed-out causes.

When I look at the white hairs I pluck out—yes, I pluck them out and do so with a *Take, that!* vigor, though I know I'm at risk of inducing baldness—I see an ugliness I would have wished not to be part of my life. UGLY—its synonyms, and it's synchronistic that (to my mind's eye) these letter-combinations seem as ugly as their meaning, are

> *horrible, despicable, reprehensible, nasty, appalling, objectionable, offensive, obnoxious, vile, dishonorable, rotten, vicious, spiteful*

After I pluck out a white hair, I usually spend several minutes contemplating it. Holding it with two fingers, I sometimes wave it as if to witness its surfing prowess with air. But, basically, I just contemplate it in silence: I don't talk to the white hair because I wish it did not exist. I just treat it with a prolonged baleful gaze. The condition precedent to each of my white hairs is suffering. What's to like?

I'm not a masochist or a martyr. I prefer Beauty to its opposite. Five years after I began plucking white hairs from my head, I decided to transform them into something I could contemplate without the pain that created them. Thus, did Art rear its pretty head.

What is hair but a line? So I thought to create drawings using hair as a line, or hairs as lines—I envisioned these drawings against dark backgrounds since I would be working with white lines. But sometime during the past several years, I also was introduced to asemics by master practitioner Tim Gaze. An "asemic" is wordless writing. Asemic artists have addressed their art in numerous ways, from writing with undefinable symbols to "found" asemics such as sidewalk cracks, patterns in nature and (as I imagine) the flow of feathers on a bird's wing.

Inspired by the early works of painter Theresa Chong who once released control to gravity for directing the flow of paint against a vertically-standing canvas, I thought to use gravity to create asemics using my white hairs. Symbolically, I wanted someone/something else to be the author so as to separate authorship from prior pain, and I chose gravity.

I saved about eight strands of hair into an envelope. I then dropped them from the envelope onto the nearest black surface I could find, which happened to be the top of a speaker attached to my computer. The hairs fell through the air and settled against the black top. I then took photographs of the results. Here are two:

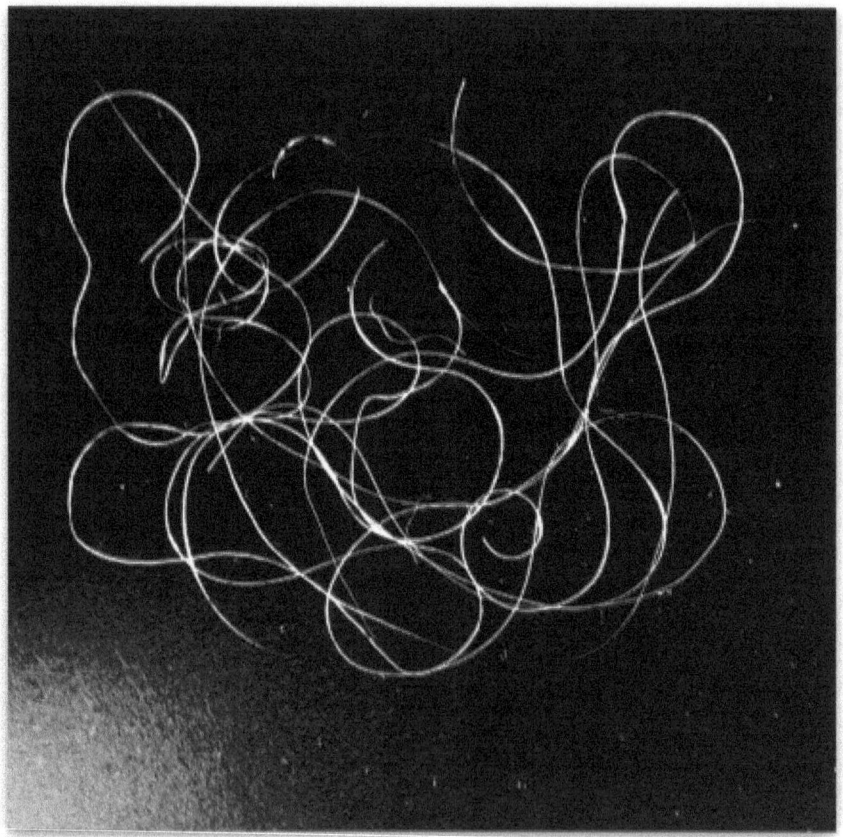

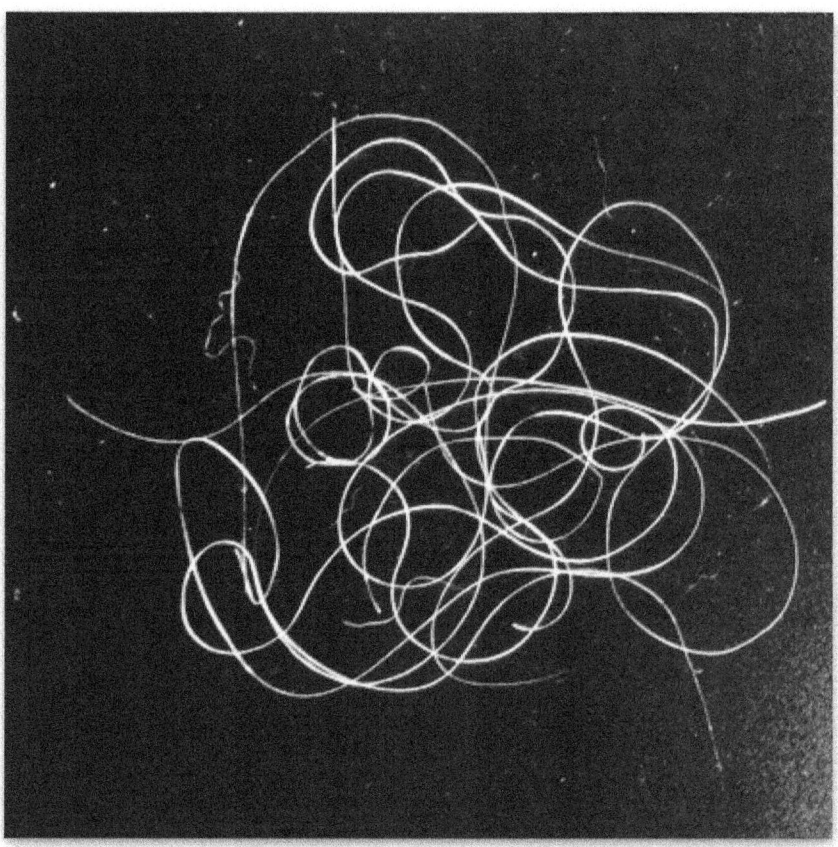

I found the effects interesting—as facilitated by the presence of dust motes atop my speaker (as a Domestic Goddess, I suck) and the glare from a nearby light, one could imagine the asemics floating in outer space. With relief, I also found the results beautiful. In becoming beautiful—and others seem to think so, too, as the first six asemics swiftly found publishers—they became pleasurable: they became the opposite of pain. Yet again, Art creates gold from brass.

Over time, the asemics would even turn feral as they seemingly mate with a petal from nearby roses (though I believe part of the images' intrigue is how the petal is not necessarily discernible as a petal):

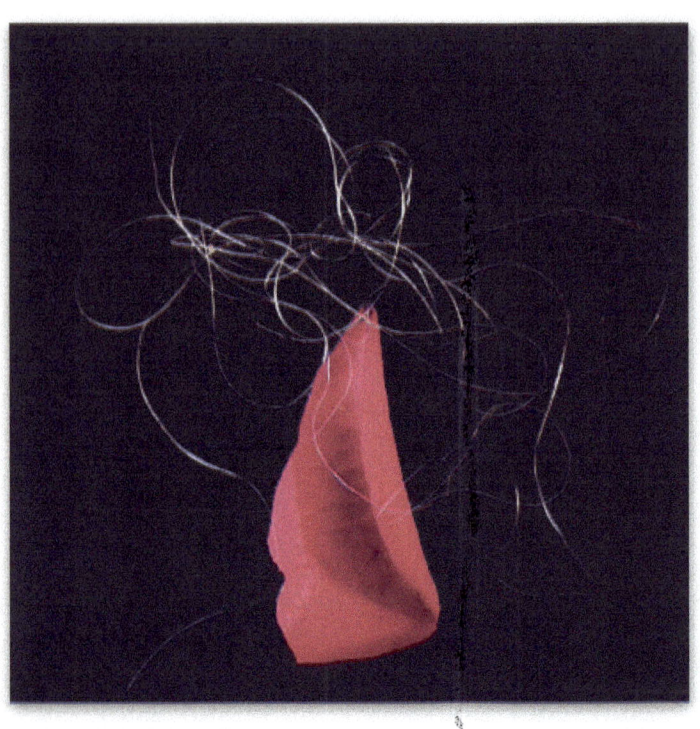
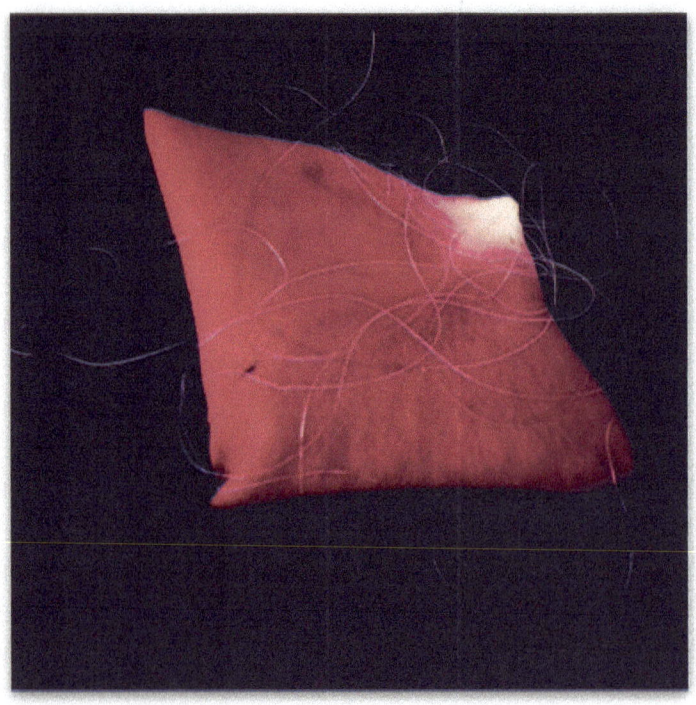

With each permutation of the dropped pattern against the speaker box—with each fall—the asemic consistently erased prior hurt, translating pain each time into pleasurable beauty. Thus, it makes sense that, most recently, the asemics, when photographed with a small rock from a birdbath, would present the story of alchemy. Here's one that the combination of camera flash and light goldened, as if touched by the mythical King Midas.

In fact, my first look at the above image made me think that not just alchemy but some sort of birthing was taking place. Perhaps the strands were locking together to birth something more solid. Or perhaps it was the other way around and the solid (rock) was emanating out the strands. In any event, a sense of narrative is presented even as it lacks a determinable plot.

Why do I consider these works asemics instead of abstract visual art? Perhaps the difference is not meaningful to some viewers. But as their conceptualizer (not author, which is gravity's role), I attest that there is a story that can be told by the white hairs, but which cannot be shared in public and consequently must remain "wordless." In the place of that story, what is presented is beauty.

One also can "deep read" the results to signify wordless perseverance despite that saying, *To Live is to Suffer*. For, soon (I hope, very soon), I have faith that the past occasions of hurt would become transformed into memories that automatically join the pain with pain's self-erasure to create

      something lovely,

      something one can contemplate without agony,

      something that evokes pleasure…

From "The Mortality Asemics (Series #1)" (2015)

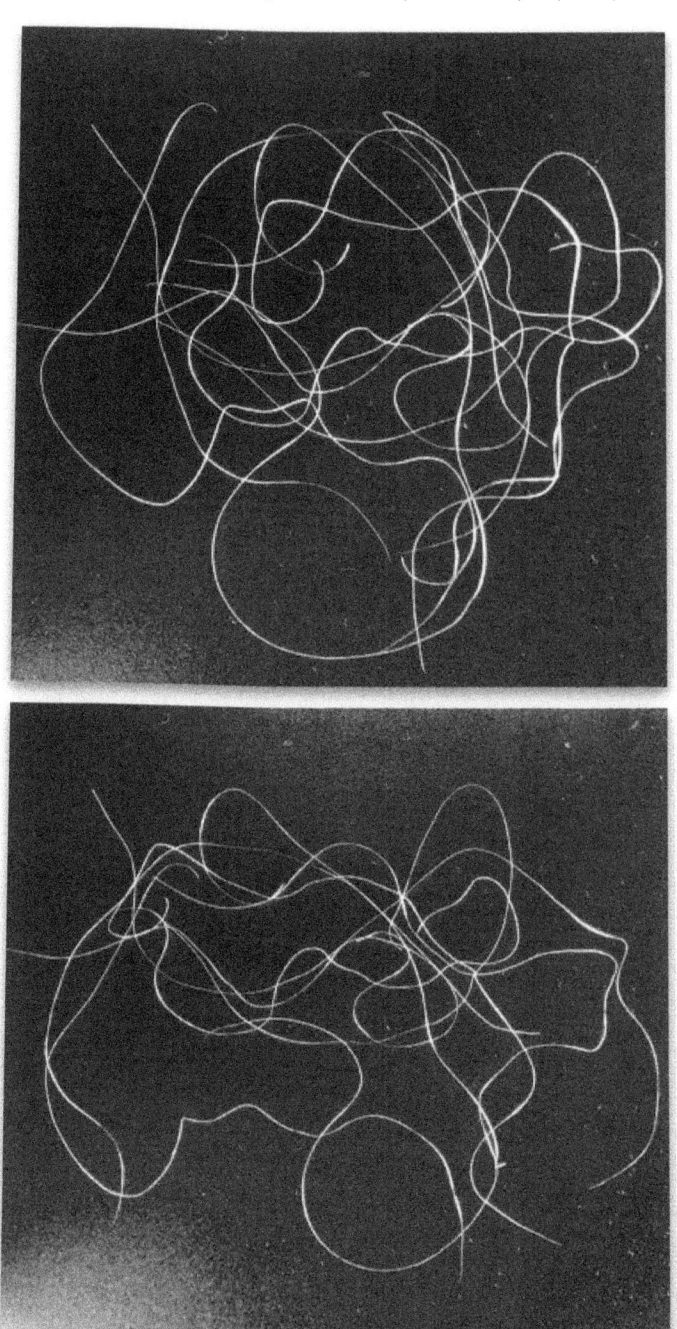

I Forget Forgetting My Skin Was Ruin (2015)

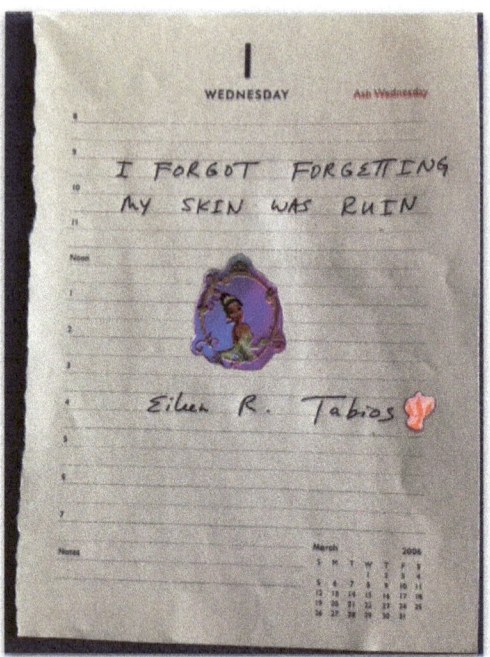

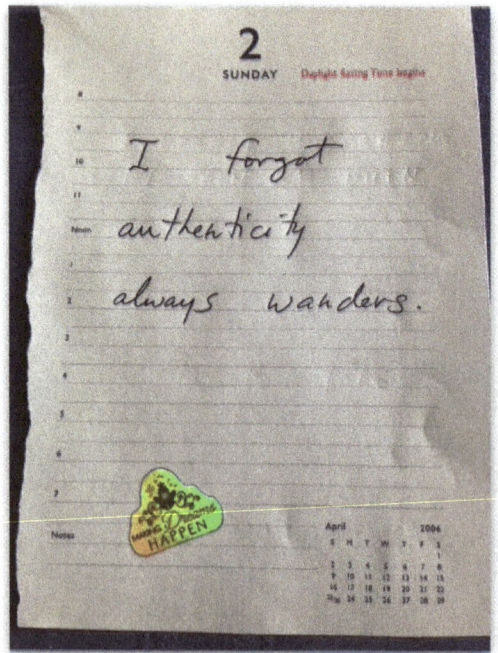

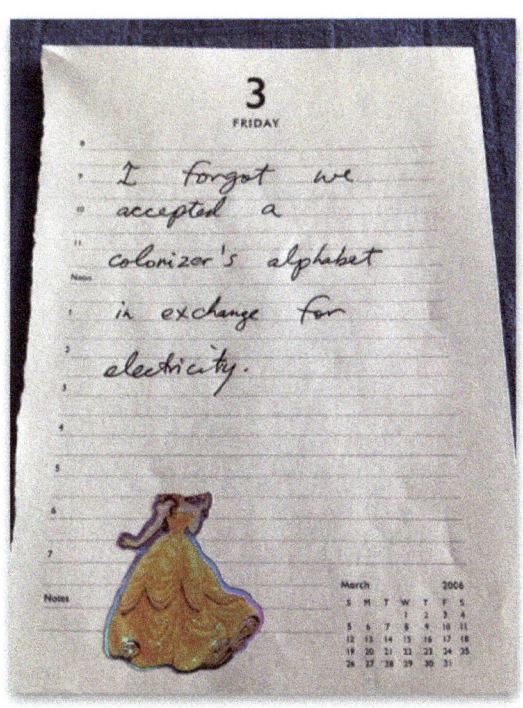

3 FRIDAY

I forgot we accepted a colonizer's alphabet in exchange for electricity.

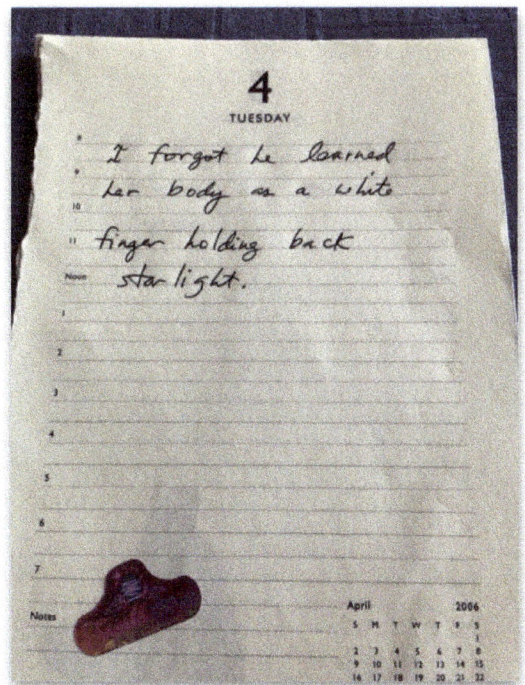

4 TUESDAY

I forgot he learned her body as a white finger holding back starlight.

I forgot symmetries
shaped by memory
lapses.

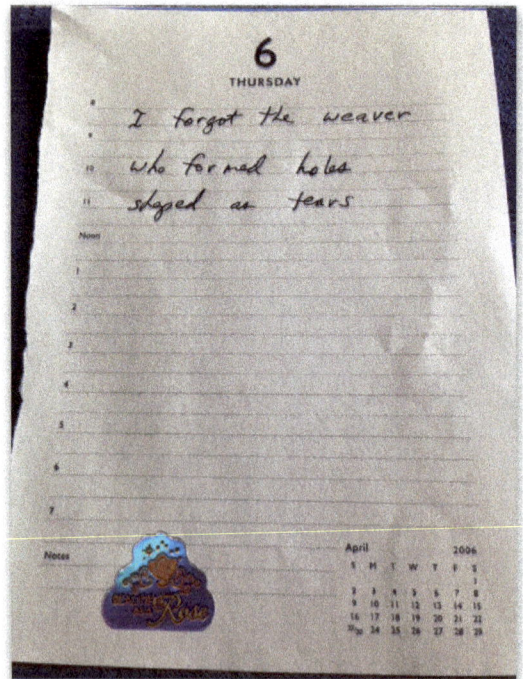

I forgot the weaver
who formed holes
shaped as tears

7
TUESDAY

I forgot preening over a labyrinth.

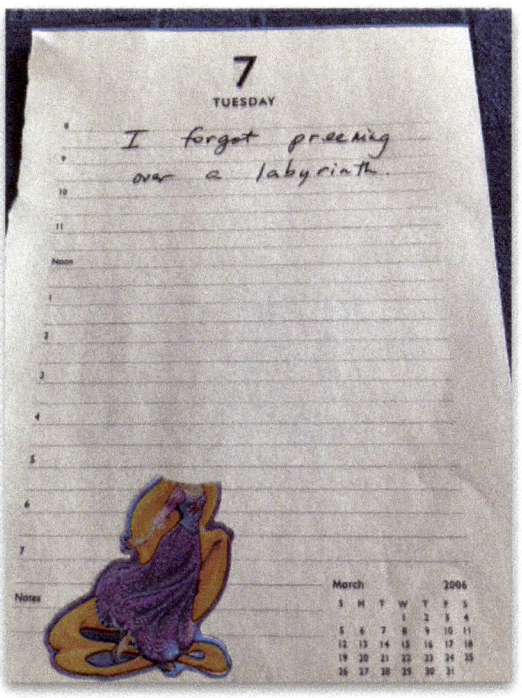

March 2006

8
SATURDAY

I forgot a girl loving marble enough to freeze into a swoon.

April 2006

Entry (2013)

THE SECRET (An Unreadable Book) (2013)

I was about to recycle these used paper towel rolls. But the Muse paused my hand and made me take a second look. After said second (then third) look, I cut off a small slice from the end of one roll:

Why did I do that? Because I remembered a review of a book I published in *Galatea Resurrects*, an online poetry review journal for which I'm editor. The book was unique in that you couldn't open it. That's right: an unopenable, thus unreadable, book. I became aware of this book, Tawrin Baker's *So That Even* (House Press, Bloomington / Buffalo / Philadelphia / New York City, 2008) through Eric Gelsinger's review (at http://galatearesurrection11.blogspot.com/2008/12/so-that-even-by-tawrin-baker.html). When you peer at the book on its side, you will see text. But the book itself can't be opened—it looks like this:

Inspired by my memories of Baker's "book," I decided to use a slice of that ex-paper towel roll to become the book cover of a similar book. Because a reader would not be able to read the book's text, I decided to use a title with the word "secret," and after much thought (at least a couple of seconds worth), I decided to title my newest book:

THE SECRET TO HAPPINESS

Then, I had to write it. I cut out a strip of paper that could later be folded within the cardboard roll. I chose a yellow-gold paper because color is a narrative (it is!) and I wanted to symbolize the Buddhist color of enlightenment. I also felt yellow and brown to be a pleasing visual combination. I also wanted to blather more on all this ... anyway:

Then, yes, I did write out the text as regards the secret to happiness:

Ooops: did the scissor inadvertently hide the secret? Sorry ... but to go on, I then inserted one end of the paper into the cardboard roll. Then I stapled one end for binding:

I stapled the other end of the cover, too, so as to prevent a reader's finger from slipping into the roll to coax out the paper bearing the secret of happiness (hah). After writing the title, the book's "front" cover looks like this:

If you look at its side profile, you will see a page whose interior text cannot be read because the book cannot be opened:

Some secrets *can* be kept.

"GIRL SINGING" (2009)

The following is the Afterword in the anthology 1000 VIEWS OF "GIRL SINGING", *Editor John Bloomberg-Rissman (Leafe Press, Nottingham, U.K., 2009).*

A (SHEEPISH) AFTERWORD

Poetry is not speech. Poetry is action. // Poems mostly don't interest me for their language—mostly, they interest me for their effect.
—from "The Blind Chatelaine's Keys" Blog, Jan. 13, 2009

Okay. While I've been flattered and honored by John Bloomberg-Rissman's choice to use my poem "The Secret Life of an Angel" as the springboard for this wonderful project, I've also been bemused. I don't really think my poem is that hot. For a poem that aspires to sing, it feels rather clunky in places.

Having said that, I can only be VERY GRATEFUL to all the participants in this anthology. Thank you for your interest, and thank you for showing how a poem can be a doorway into something far larger than anything an author could have intended or anticipated. By doing so, you all show why Poetry is *marvelous*!

However, I didn't just admire the transformations taken by this book's participants. I was also shamed into attempting to "improve" my original poem. It was unexpectedly complicated to do so since I was no longer in the "space" in which I first created the poem. But I didn't let that stop me for, the other writers were never in that space! Here, then, is my own textual transformation of my original version—this version uses the form of a hay(na)ku sequence:

ANTI-WINTER: THE DOUBLE LIFE OF AN ANGEL
—after Eileen Tabios' "The Secret Life of An Angel" after Jose Garcia Villa's "Girl Singing"

Girl singing. Day.
Winter's old
man

reaches for immortality
with a
lengthening

shadow despite my
skipping
away.

Girl singing! I
insist. Day!
Cheerfully

chant to keep
the clouds
from

dimming the sun,
from milking
skies

of their cobalt
gazes bespeaking
purity.

He has worn
many guises,
and

I have let him:
the original
angel

who fell and
fell—"glorious
ride,"

he has whispered
for his
spell.

"This is a
game of
poker

I have lost,
but no
longer

wish to play,"
I reply.
Girl

singing. Day! I
proclaim: "You
cannot

scoff, my secret
demon. For
I

played with high
stakes while
you

merely watched." Girl
singing. Day.
I

risked everything while
you hedged.
I

sang notes only
virgin boys
can

muster, only fearful
dogs can
hear.

I lost myself
in everyone's
"valley

of evil" but
my wings
unfurled

to make me
rise. Unlike
your

wings, mine did
not betray. Girl
singing.

Day. Beloved wings
unfurled as
I

changed my mind
for Heaven
nearer

than mere breath
away. Girl
singing:

> *Day...oh. Daaaaaaaaay...oh. Girl*
> *go singing*
> *Daaaaaaaaaaayay....oh!*

The last paragraph was created to reflect a sense of Jamaican music, a thought inspired by a conversation with Tim Gaze over sound poetry. At the time I rewrote my poem, I was discussing with Tim his brilliant book, *NOOLOGY*,
which addresses glitchy (choppy, lurching electronic sound) visual poetry.

But perhaps I name-drop Tim Gaze to seem smarter than I am, because I still was not fully satisfied with my new text-version of the poem. This version, however, felt as if it's as far as I could take it through words. Thus, I decided to do another version, but this time through visual art. Here is a "hay(na)ku collage" version of the poem, created from elements of three advertisements (reflecting the three lines of a hay(na)ku stanza) ripped from the *New York Times Sunday Magazine*:

Well, as my no-nonsense husband shared about my collage, I "pose no threat to Jess or Rauschenberg." But if the above image still accomplishes less than the proverbial effect of a (magnificent) thousand words, then perhaps such a flaw is finally the appropriate place to leave this poem. For it occurs to me, too, that my original poem is a manifestation of a wabi-sabi approach that's long been a poetics interest. It is often through the flaw that the artist creates a space for others. Here, what is important is not "my" poem but others' poems. I am grateful that one of my poems inspired them to respond with new poems.

I am blessed that my poem's "others" have been so loving. Thank you John Bloomberg-Rissman and everyone in this book.

Eileen Tabios
January 14, 2009
St. Helena, CA

Poem-Sculpture Collaborations with Nick Carbo (2005)

The collaboration between Nick Carbó and Eileen R. Tabios unfolded through snailmail, with each sending a sculpture that generates a poem. Unfortunately, it's not possible to share images of all of the described sculptures as they were damaged in a flood. The exception is the first image. But what's poetry for but not an exercise of the imagination? Perhaps the reader can imagine the other images based on their descriptions. Meanwhile, the collaboration unfolded as follows:

1) Nick sends a sculpture comprised of a toilet regulator painted with the following words:

> Can you regulate
> The flow of desire

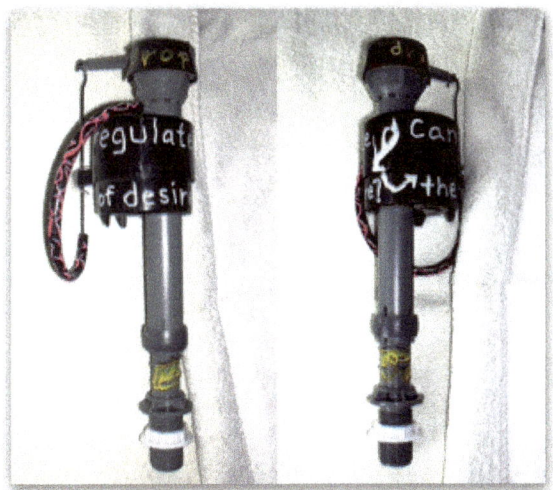

2) Eileen responds by sending a wooden box recycled from one containing wine bottles of Screaming Eagle. The phrase "Screaming Eagle" is emblazoned, along with the image of an eagle in flight, against the box. The box contains long ribbons designed to spill forth when the box is opened. Attached to the side of a box is a toilet's flusher mechanism. The accompanying poem:

> Trap the intangible
> to release
> Desire most beautiful
> when unleashed

3) Nick replies by sending a blue box containing Alka Selzer tablets upon which are incribed letters. When the box is opened, the tablets spell out the following poem:

Take one Saussarian pill 3X daily to induce / Desire
This is how the cerulean curve
of her spine presents pink
ideas at four in the afternoon
where words become
arbitrary trees, cones
intangible blues
This is how the
release feels at the tip
of the tongue when pressed
against his wet
red frenulum slippery
with meaning

4) Eileen responds by sending four stacking boxes, correlated to four stanzas of a poem. Each stanza is written on the inside cover of a box. Boxes are colored blue and white and stacked atop each other with a white ribbon tying them together. All must be unwrapped in order to go through sculpture. Eileen very much wanted to include (the bodies of) the audience (reader/viewer) into the sculpture by having their involvement through the process of unwrapping the boxes.

The first box contains a pearl necklace cellophane-wrapped in its middle so that it's not possible to wear it. The second box contains an American Red Cross pin referencing breast cancer. The third box contains used ribbons from unwrapped gifts. The fourth box contains a grey sports bra overlaid with a pretty lacey bra.
Inside the fourth box, the stanza is encompassed within a circle, as formed by a "Filipino poet" symbol's belly (from an earlier project by Eileen Tabios entitled "Poems Form/From The Six Directions"). The bras are "convex with concave." Here's the accompanying poem:

Untitled

Surely we
Never wish

To stray
From bodies

Those curves
Offering possibilities

For
"the convex with the concave"

Global Warming (2009)

Artist Notes:

Nota Bene Eiswein's front cover image is the collage "Global Warming" (2008) which was inspired by the heat of flamenco, a photograph of the Barne Glacier by Seth White, and asemic writing practices to which I was introduced by Tim Gaze. The asemic portion of the collage utilizes a symbol for "Filipino poet" as created through the author's 2001-2002 "Poems Form/From The Six Directions" project. Also relevant to this collage as well as the underlying sensibility to these poems is an observation by Christian Dotremont:

> *"The printed sentence is like a city map: the bushes, trees, objects, and myself have disappeared."*

Listing Poem Towards The New Filipino Society (2007)

I was honored to be among over 50 Filipino poets, artists, writers, and poet-artists from around the world who participated in "Chromatext Reloaded," curated by Sid Gomez Hildawa, Jean Marie Syjuco and Alfred Yuson, and held at the Main Gallery of the Cultural Center of the Philippines.

My contribution was a visual poetry installation entitled "List(ing) Poem: Towards The New Filipino Society". The core of the installation is a "list poem" with each line the title of a book by Ferdinand Marcos. As I was born in the Philippines in 1960, the former dictator's legacy informs me and my family history. I would like to share the conceptual underpinnings to this work:

The installation includes five pieces of drawings/collages. They are intended to hang to form or reference a cross (Drawings Nos. 1 and 2 to be on either side of the three drawings—Nos. 3, 4 and 5—lined up vertically). The design evokes crucifixion—for "Eileen R. Tabios" or Filipinos were sacrificed (crucified) by the Marcos' dictatorship. Although the drawings can hang against a wall, they ideally would be pinned—still in the cross shape—against a red lush fabric (red velvet or red silk or red satin) because red denotes the color of blood.

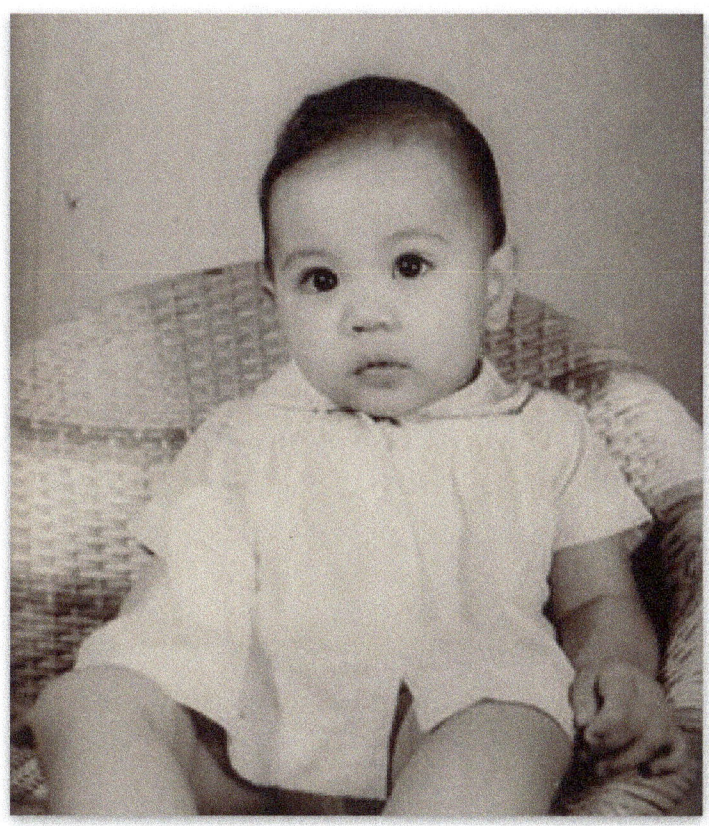

Drawings Nos. 1 and 2 feature a print-out of the poem ripped apart to show my baby photo. Such denotes how I was part of the multitudes affected—and ripped apart—by the Marcos' reign. Also pasted are stickers of tsinelas, or flip-flops, a common footwear in the Philippines. I also conceived of the "rip" as the ripping out of Filipinos into the diaspora—in Drawing No. 4, the tsinelas are supposed to be walking away from the Philippines (or from the baby as I lived in the Philippines as a child).

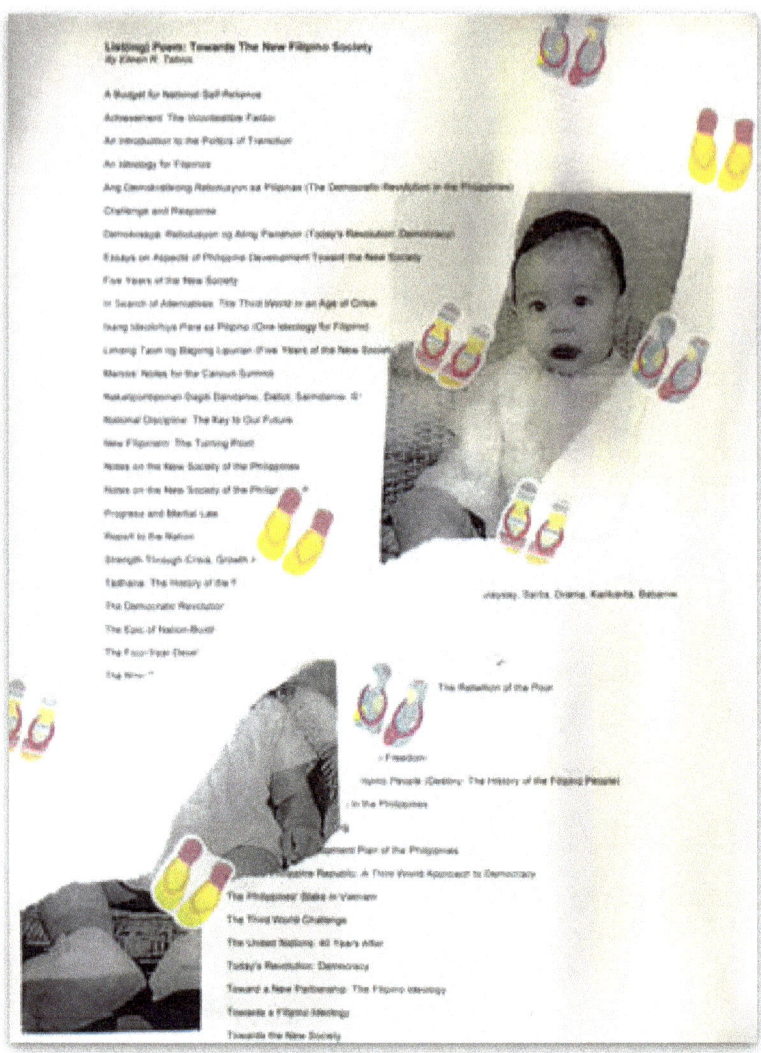

Drawing No. 1 also features in the bottom right corner some "ascemic" poetry created by me writing out my name and then writing "Marcos" over my name so that the result is not legible (asemic).

The tsinelas stickers are first pasted in Drawing No. 3, before continuing downward on to Drawing No. 4. The first tsinelas sticker is aligned with the 10-11th line to reference my departing from the Philippines at age 10.

Drawings No. 3 and 4 feature my handwriting of the poem. There are the same number of lines as in the poem itself. But each line, in red ink, was hand-written as "Eileen R. Tabios." As of the 11th line, "Marcos" is handwritten over each line of my name. This symbolizes how I grew up outside the Philippines as of age 11. As time unfolds (as of Drawing No. 4), the "Marcos" becomes black marker ink to emphasize the editing out cum erasure of "Eileen R. Tabios." This references how the Marcos regime snuffed out the future of (or a certain better future for) many Filipinos.

The color red is initially used for handwriting the ascemic text because red evokes blood. When, in Drawing No. 4, the red changes to black (the ink color in most of my pens), the switch is to symbolize how life becomes a poem—I live out my poems before I write them.

Drawing No. 5 shows a blank page, except for the bottom line of "Poe[m]" melting into my name. This symbolizes how the final (if there is a final) legacy of the Marcos dictatorship has yet to be written, but that the poet (or poem)—not the dictator—will have the last word.

૨઼ ૨઼ ૨઼

In a follow-up email, curator Alfred A. Yuson asked whether, in mailing my drawings to Manila, I placed the works between thick cardboard to prevent them from wrinkling. I replied, "They may get bent or folded but that could be fixed by you either framing them or temporarily placing them beneath some heavy books. But, frankly, if they come wrinkled or in messed up shape, that's OKAY with me, and feel free to hang them in that condition. That would fit my poetics of a poem being effective when it's 'used', or engaged with by the audience—even the blind audience of a postal system...."

I also suggested that the curators consider putting lechon, a suckling pig, on a table in front of and beneath the drawings—with an American red apple in its mouth. Such would evoke the involvement—the support—of past U.S. policies to the Marcos dictatorship. I added that the idea might be a good one since, during the exhibition opening, attendees then could eat from the lechon. Mr. Yuson didn't think the idea feasible since the opening's attendees would include Moslems. I didn't quibble with his response since it manifested respect for some of the anticipated visitors. In conceptualizing this installation, I thought it great that, unlike with how the Marcos reign unfolded, *Respect* would have the last word.

૨઼ ૨઼ ૨઼

The following is the text version of my poem. I feel that to read each line, knowing that each line is the title of a book penned by Ferdinand M. Marcos, is to highlight the tragedy of how much potential the Philippines has lost as a result of corrupt politics:

List(ing) Poem: Towards The New Filipino Society

A Budget for National Self-Reliance

Achievement: The Incontestible Factor

An Introduction to the Politics of Transition

An Ideology for Filipinos

Ang Demokratikong Rebolusyon sa Pilipinas (The Democratic Revolution in the Philippines)

Challenge and Response

Demokrasya: Rebolusyon ng Ating Panahon (Today's Revolution: Democracy)

Essays on Aspects of Philippine Development Toward the New Society
Five Years of the New Society

In Search of Alternatives: The Third World in an Age of Crisis

Isang Ideolohiya Para sa Pilipino (One Ideology for Filipino)

Limang Taon ng Bagong Lipunan (Five Years of the New Society)

Marcos' Notes for the Cancun Summit

Nakatipontiponan Dagiti Dandaniw, Dallot, Sarindaniw, Salaysay, Sarita, Drama, Kankanta, Babaniw

National Discipline: The Key to Our Future

New Filipinism: The Turning Point

Notes on the New Society of the Philippines

Notes on the New Society of the Philippines II: The Rebellion of the Poor

Progress and Martial Law

Report to the Nation

Strength Through Crisis, Growth in Freedom

Tadhana: The History of the Filipino People (Destiny: The History of the Filipino People)

The Democratic Revolution in the Philippines

The Epic of Nation-Building

The Four-Year Development Plan of the Philippines

The New Philippine Republic: A Third World Approach to Democracy

The Philippines ' Stake in Vietnam

The Third World Challenge

The United Nations: 40 Years After

Today's Revolution: Democracy

Toward a New Partnership: The Filipino Ideology

Towards a Filipino Ideology

Towards the New Society

The Corporate Cat (2007)

The process was of randomly grabbing …

(then buying) three sets …

of stickers from a store display …

The goal was to juxtapose what had been …

consciously-unrelated themes, as presented…

by the stickers, into (visual) poems …

The faith was that it will happen …

The conclusion was that it happened …

because poetry is all around us and ...

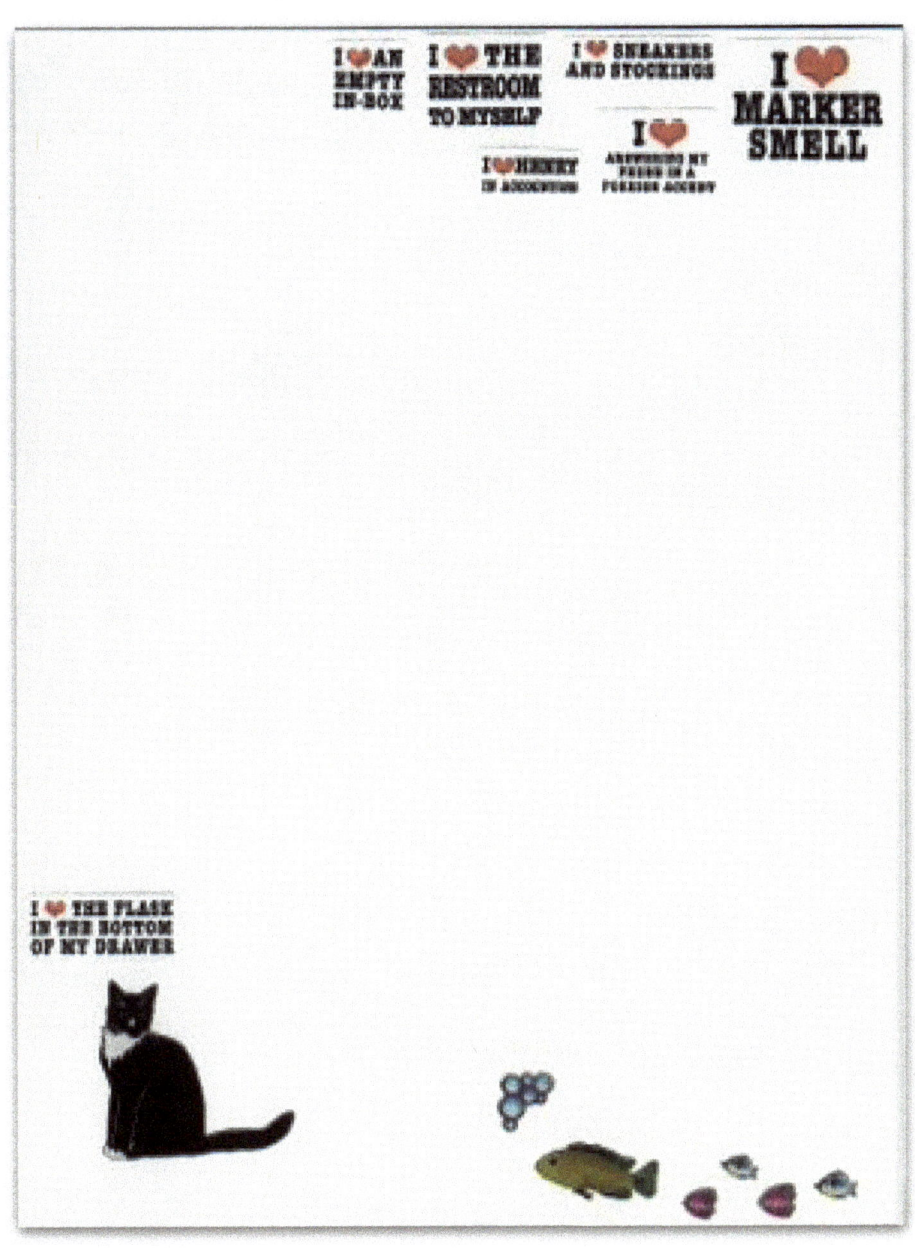

sometimes, the poet need only choose to see ...

P.S. The preference is multi-layered poetry and I consider this series also to be drawings of "white space."

GRIDS (2007)
—*a "chained hay(na)ku" created while reading Michelle Naka Pierce's* BELOVED INTEGER

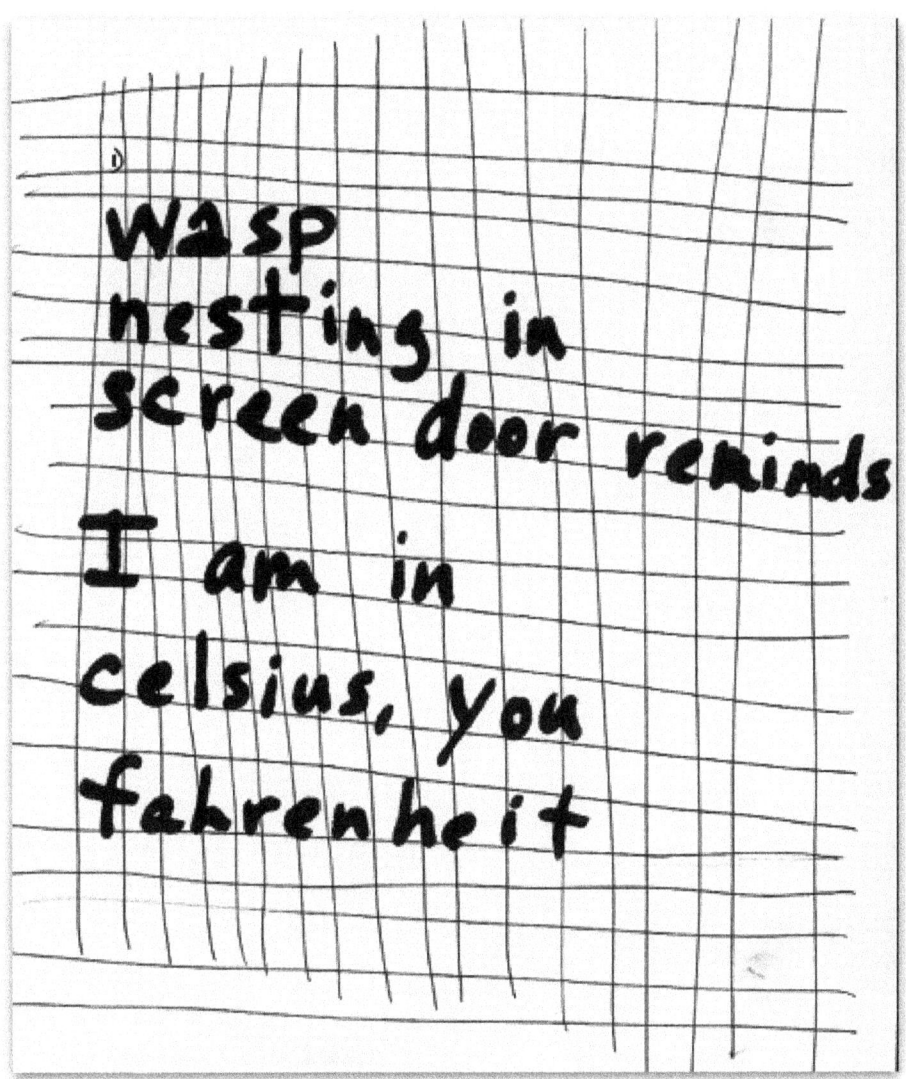

2)

Physics posits two objects cannot inhabit the same space. Thus, I write US.

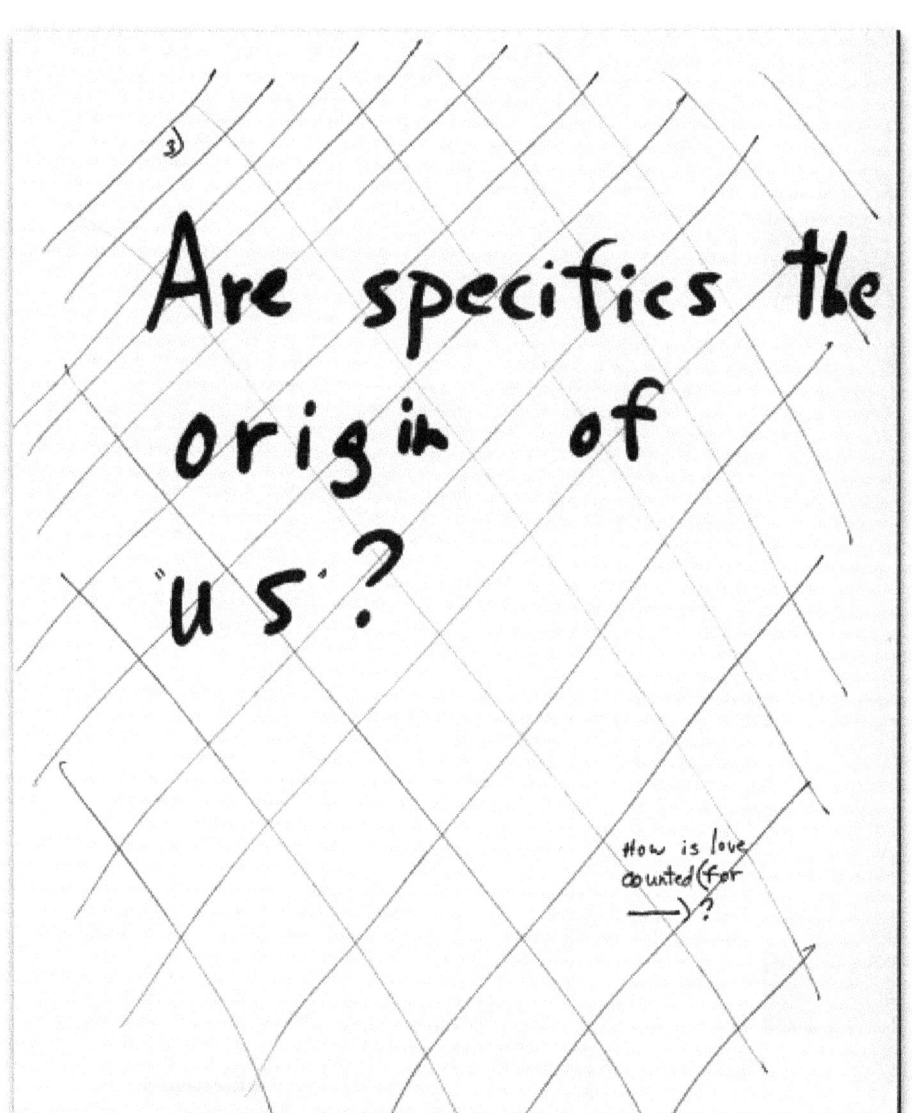

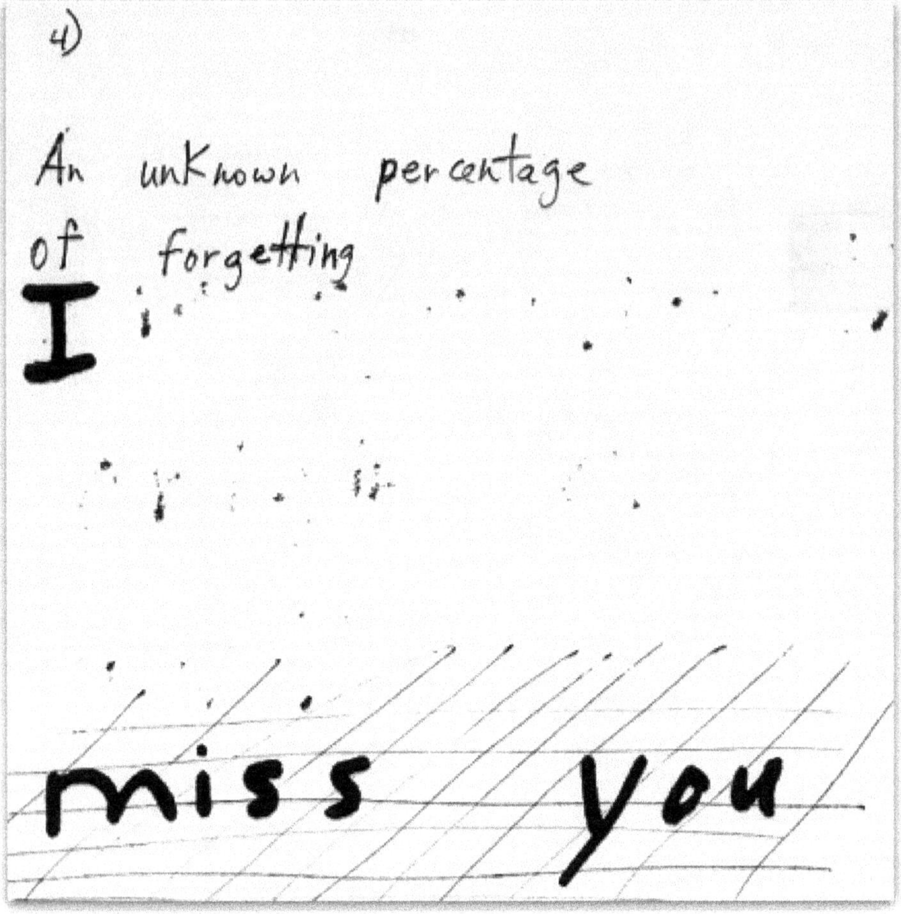

4)

An unknown percentage
of forgetting
I

miss you

5)

~~How~~
did we
come to this—

finding
each other

through writing poems?

Not to say
I find
myself

HERE. I do

find that
portion

of myself who
occupies that
SpaceWeCallUS.

6.
CONCLUSION MASQUERADING AS POSTSCRIPT

Barry shares an April 6, 2004 article from The Guardian which partly *says*

Scientists examining what
they thought
were

Petrarch's remains discovered
the skull
belongs

to someone else.
And they
suspect

it could be
that of
Eve—

the nickname for
every woman
designated

by history to
be *Miss
Anonymous.*

You read a poem to make everything WHOLE

I, ergo, write ~~poem~~ fragmentation of shadow

A Feminist Can Make Achilles Heel (2006)

THE SECRET LIVES OF PUNCTUATIONS (2006)

Mixed Media (cut-up postcard from The Peninsula, a New York City hotel; Singer brass snap fasteners; Scotch tape; red and blue ink) 5 x 7" (2005)

Artist Statement:
I thought to create a postcard image that manifested the theme of my poetry collection *THE SECRET LIVES OF PUNCTUATIONS, VOL. I.*

I chose a postcard from a hotel because trysts, a form of secrets, can be held in hotels. I cut a strip from the bottom of the original card to size it at 5 X 7", one of the two sizes allowed for becoming part of the 2006 INTERNATIONAL

HAND MADE POSTCARD EXHIBITION (IHMP Exhibition) in Kuala Lumpur, Malaysia.

I then divided the sliced-off strip into five portions, atop of which I wrote five punctuations addressed in my book: colon, semi-colon, parenthesis, question mark and ellipsis. I chose red ink to feature the punctuations as red is the color for passion...and lipstick.

Using a snap fastener, I pinned each of these symbolized punctuations to one of the hotel rooms of the hotel. There is a sixth snap-on fastener missing a punctuation, both to symbolize "secret" and to reference one of the punctuations not represented from my book: the strike-through.

I used snap fasteners to pin the punctuations against hotel rooms because these fasteners are usually used in clothing. So to unsnap or snap them references undressing and dressing—activities relevant to (secret) trysts.

I also used the snap fasteners in a reverse way; the back—not the front—of the fasteners are what's visible, again to reference secrets in that the "normal" public façade of the object has been subverted or masked.

In addition, I made visible the back components of the snap fastener because I actually found them more pleasing to the eye—which is to say, more appropriate from a formal (sculptural) point of view and to imply that the secrets of punctuations provide pleasure. The latter element is significant since the work refers to a poetry book and it is my ideal that poems give pleasure to their readers or viewers.

I wrote the title atop the postcard, then placed scotch tape across the title. I did so to prevent the ink from further bleeding, as well as to reference how the ink is now "masked" by tape. Of course the text is visible from beneath the mask/tape. The visibility of secrets relates to the revelations of which punctuation is unfolding its secret within which hotel room.

Those involved in secret hotel trysts rarely send out postcards about their acts. But because my poetry collection reveals "the secrets of punctuations," I also thought the postcard medium to be appropriate for it proclaims a message to the world. Specifically, even if a postcard is mailed to a specific recipient, the fact that its message is not hidden from postal service workers and others who may see it means that its message is "public."

Relatedly, I intend for my poems to be "postcards" to the entire universe.

From "POEMS FORM/FROM THE SIX DIRECTIONS" (2001-2002)

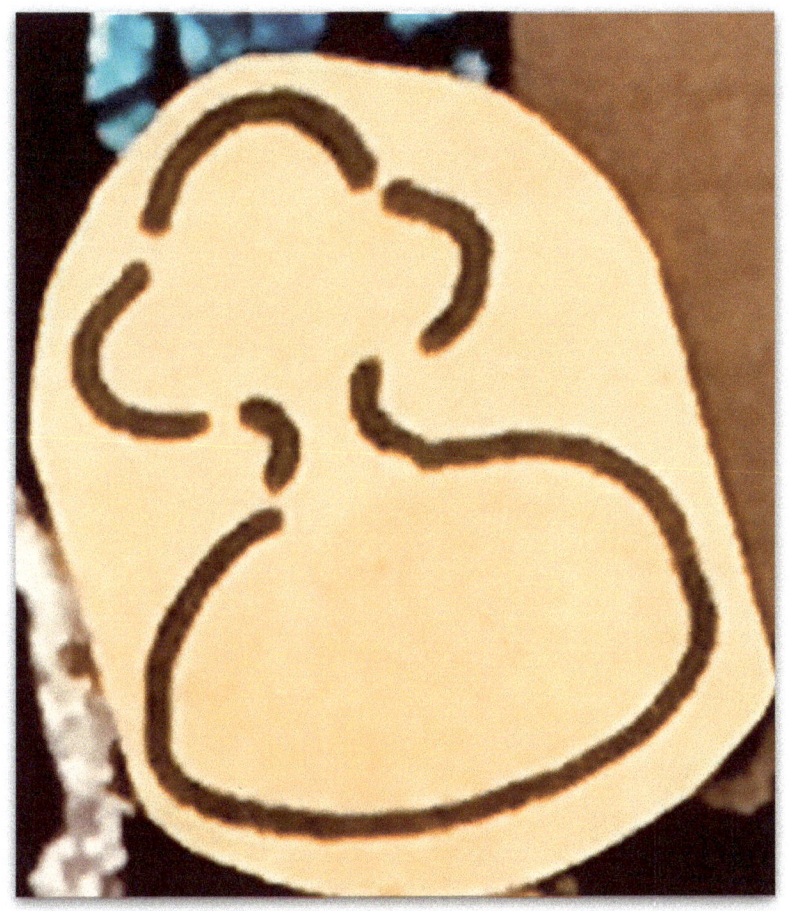

"As a writer working mostly with imagination and words, I experienced a pleasurable frisson in feeling the tangibility of the found materials that made their way into my sculptures (e.g. old coasters, used magazines, ribbons, used cardboard and so on). The sculpting process for Six Directions created a simmer in my belly, similar to the physical effect that I often feel when I can feel myself successfully chasing down a poem into a verse. I, therefore, decided to try my own hand at working as a visual artist. I hadn't planned to go this route, but I allowed myself to follow the impulse as I realized that this opening manifested what is also wonderful about all Art and Poetry: that is, how they can lead its maker and viewer/reader into new experiences.

"I began by simply trying to draw. Because I was new at this, I didn't have any drawing-related materials like sketching pads. I began by drawing on what was available to me: brown paper bags that were piling up in my kitchen. I also

appreciated the use of the paper bags because they are found objects. As with the found material that comprised my earlier sculptures, the inclusion of found objects symbolize how I integrate (elements of) the world into my work. The paper bags came to form a visual art installation, 'The Brown Paper Bag Series,' consisting of 19 paper bag drawings hung together as a group....

"By evoking the notion of Filipino kayumanggi *skin, the brown color of the paper bags had caused me to view the installation as a way to explore my identity as a Filipino/a poet. The early drawings show me drawing a circle because it is a simple image. However, I was uneasy with the circle because I related it more to the* enso, *the Japanese word for circle. I didn't yet know what the* enso *had to do with me (except for providing an archetypal image that I love). This also explains why one drawing incorporates a xeroxed photo of me when I was still in college: to show my less mature self who had not yet began to address issues of identity.*

"Later drawings, however, show the transformation of the circle into an abstracted outline of a vegetable gourd (this abstract icon is essentially a small circle atop a larger circle). The gourd image references an Ilokano indigenous myth that describes how the first human came out of a cracked gourd. For me, the gourd image came to symbolize 'Filipino/a poet,' as reflected in the drawings that conclude the series. It is worth noting, however, that my gourd icon did not erase but only incorporated the reference to the enso. *This is significant because I believe that the exploration of one's identity or culture is not synonymous with rejecting other cultures.*

Creating 'The Brown Paper Bag Series' led me to making other drawings where my drawing 'mark' is consistently the gourd icon (for instance, if I drew a horizon, I would use tiny gourd images lined up closely together to form a horizontal line)....
—*from "Poems Form/From The Six Directions,"* **Our Own Voice***, 2002*

"POEMS FORM/FROM THE SIX DIRECTIONS" generated sculptures, drawings, mixed media collages, an installation exhibit, collaborations with other artists, and various performance happenings in San Francisco, Santa Rosa and Berkeley. The following are images featuring the gourd image symbolizing "Filipino/a poet" in the poet's "marriage" to Poetry:

This theme was further solidified in the 2005 book *I TAKE THEE, ENGLISH, FOR MY BELOVED* (Marsh Hawk Press, 2005):

Six Directions Drawing #2

Six Directions Drawing #13

ACKNOWLEDGEMENTS

Deep gratitude to the editors, curators, and publishers of the following publications and spaces that first featured individual works from this collection:

Facebook hashtag #thebigboxstorepoetryproject curated by Pamela Hart: "Arrival: An Impossibility" (2016)

1000 VIEWS OF "GIRL SINGING", Editor John Bloomberg-Rissman (Leafe Press, Nottingham, U.K., 2009): "GIRL SINGING" (2009), as well as the Afterword and referenced poem, *"ANTI-WINTER: THE DOUBLE LIFE OF AN ANGEL"*

2006 INTERNATIONAL HAND MADE POSTCARD EXHIBITION curated by Suzlee Ibrahim and Nalur Seni at the Garden of Art, in collaboration with ARTPROJECT2006, in Kuala Lumpur, Malaysia: "The Secret Lives of Punctuations" (2006)

Berfrois, Editor Russell Bennetts: "Witnessed in the Convex Mirror: Tense Past Tense / Tanka #160"

"CHROMATEXT REBOOTED" curated by Jean Marie Syjuco and Alfred A. Yuson, Cultural Center of the Philippines (Manila), 2015-2016: "DON'T CALL ME FILIPINO" (2015)

"CHROMATEXT RELOADED," an exhibition curated by Sid Hildawa, Jean Marie Syjuco and Alfred A. Yuson; sponsored by the Philippine Literary Arts Council; and held at the Cultural Center of the Philippines (Manila), 2007: "LISTING POEM: TOWARDS THE NEW FILIPINO SOCIETY" (2007)

Datableed, Editors Eleanor Perry and Juha Virtanen: "Witnessed in the Convex Mirror (#23) / Tanka #159"

E-Ratio, Editor Gregory Vincent St. Thomasino: "Witnessed in the Convex Mirror #27): Beyond the Stars / Tanka #148"; "Witnessed in the Convex Mirror (#16): Blind Physicists / Tanka #149"; and "Witnessed in the Convex Mirror (#59) / Tanka #150"

Evening Will Come: A Monthly Journal of Poetics (Issue 33)—Women of Visual Poetry Issue, Editor Jessica Smith: "Entry" (2013)

EVIDENCE OF FETUS DIVERSITY, Editor Eileen R. Tabios (Moria Books' Locofo Chaps, Chicago, 2018): "Colonial Mentality"

EXCAVATING THE FILIPINO IN ME by Eileen R. Tabios (Tinfish, Hawai'I, 2016): "DON'T CALL ME FILIPINO" (2015)

"FACING FEMINISM" curated by Annette Marie Hyder (The McKnight Foundation and Walker Art Center): "A Feminist Can Make Achilles Heel" (2006)

Fieralingue, Editor Anny Ballardini: *"ANTI-WINTER: THE DOUBLE LIFE OF AN ANGEL"*

h&, a journal of visual/concrete poetry curated by Ian Whistle: From "The Limits of CLOUDYGENOUS" (2018); "MY ADOPTION" (2018); "I Recall Forgetting A Secret From My Youth" (2018); "Erasing Amnesia" (2018); "KOMMAS: A Speculative Fiction" (2016); "Excerpt from the Novelist's Diary (2016); "Mooring After Loss" (2016); "The Great American Novel" (2016); "For Christmas, the Hay(na)ku Visits Serbia" (2015); "The Outsider's Dilemma" (2015); and "I Forget Forgetting My Skin Was Ruin" (2015)

I TAKE THEE, ENGLISH, FOR MY BELOVED by Eileen R. Tabios (Marsh Hawk Press, New York, 2005) whose front cover was designed by Claudia Carlson: "POEMS FORM/FROM THE SIX DIRECTIONS" (2002)

Nota Bene Eiswein by Eileen R. Tabios (Ahadada Books, Tokyo & Toronto, 2009): "Global Warming" (2009)

Otoliths, Editor Mark H. Young: "CLOUDYGENOUS ARS POETICA (2018); "Community of Vowels" (2018); "The Mortality Asemics" (Series #3) (2015); "The Corporate Cat" (2007); and "GRIDS" (2007)

Our Own Voice, Editor Reme Grefalda: "POEMS FORM/FROM THE SIX DIRECTIONS" (2002) and "LISTING POEM: TOWARDS THE NEW FILIPINO SOCIETY" (2007)

qarrtsiluni, Jan. 23, 2009, Editor Dave Bonta: "Poem-Sculpture Collaborations with Nick Carbo" (2005)

Queen Mob's Teahouse, Editor Reb Livingston: "The Mortality Asemics" (Series #2) (2015)

Rigorous, Vol. Two, Issue 1, Editors Rosalyn Spencer, Kenyatta JP Garcia, Carla Williams, and Jonathan Penton: "Translation: Colonialism" (2018)

SitWithMoi Blog: "THE SECRET (An Unreadable Book)" (2013)

TANKA, VOL. I by Eileen R. Tabios (Simulacrum Press, Ontario, Canada, 2018): From "The MDR Poetry Generator: RE-MEMBER-ING TANKA (#10)"

The Big Box Poetry Project curated by Pamela Hart: "Arrival: An Impossibility" (2016)

THE LIGHT SANG AS IT LEFT YOUR EYES: Our Autobiography by Eileen R. Tabios (Marsh Hawk Press, New York, 2007): "LISTING POEM: TOWARDS THE NEW FILIPINO SOCIETY" (2007); and "The Corporate Cat" (2007)

The New Post-Literate: A Gallery of Asemic Writing curated by Michael Jacobson: "The Mortality Asemics" (Series #1) (2015)

THE SECRET LIVES OF PUNCTUATIONS, VOL. I by Eileen R. Tabios (xPress(ed), Espoo, Finland, 2006): "The Secret Lives of Punctuations" (2006)

Timglaset (Malmo, Sweden, 2019): "Six Directions Drawing #2" and "Six Directions Drawing #13" (2002)

Verity La, Managing Editor Michele Seminara: "From "PILIPINZ CLOUDYGENOUS" (2018-2019)"

"World Association of Visual and Experimental Artists," an international mail art exhibit, Curator Dejan Bogojevic, 19 Club National Mussuem Valjevo, Serbia: "The Hay(na)ku Visits Serbia" (2015)

ABOUT THE POET

(Photo-Treatment by Aileen Ibardaloza-Cassinetto)

Eileen R. Tabios loves books and has released over 50 collections of poetry, fiction, essays, and experimental biographies from publishers in nine countries and cyberspace. She is the inventor of the poetry form "hay(na)ku" whose 15-year anniversary in 2018 was celebrated in the United States with exhibitions and readings at the San Francisco Public Library and Saint Helena Public Library. Translated into nine languages, she also has edited, co-edited or conceptualized 15 anthologies of poetry, fiction and essays as well as served as editor or guest editor for various literary journals. Her writing and editing works have received recognition through awards, grants and residencies. More information is available at http://eileenrtabios.com

Established in 2016, PALOMA PRESS is a San Francisco Bay Area-based independent literary press publishing poetry, prose, and limited edition books. PALOMA PRESS believes in the power of the literary arts, how it can create empathy, bridge divides, change the world. To this end, Paloma has released fundraising chapbooks such as *MARAWI*, in support of relief efforts in the Southern Philippines; and *AFTER IRMA AFTER HARVEY*, in support of hurricane-displaced animals in Texas, Florida and Puerto Rico. As part of the San Francisco Litquake Festival, Paloma proudly curated the wildly successful literary reading, "THREE SHEETS TO THE WIND," and raised money for the Napa Valley Community Disaster Relief Fund. In 2018, the fundraising anthology, *HUMANITY*, was released in support of UNICEF's Emergency Relief campaigns on the borders of the United States and in Syria.

www.ingramcontent.com/pod-product-compliance
Lightning Source LLC
Chambersburg PA
CBHW061221070526
44584CB00029B/3926